Essential Histories

The Gulf War 1991

Essential Histories

The Gulf War 1991

Alastair Finlan

First published in Great Britain in 2003 by Osprey Publishing,
Elms Court, Chapel Way, Botley, Oxford OX2 9LP
Email: info@ospreypublishing.com

Every attempt has been made by the Publishers to secure the
appropriate permissions for material reproduced in this book. If
there has been any oversight we will be happy to rectify the
situation and written submissions should be made to the
Publishers.

ISBN 1 84176 574 0

A CIP catalogue record for this book is available from the
British Library

Editor: Sally Rawlings
Design: Ken Vail Graphic Design, Cambridge, UK
Cartography by The Map Studio
Index by Alison Worthington
Picture research by Image Select International
Origination by Grasmere Digital Imaging, Leeds, UK
Printed and bound in China by L. Rex Printing Company Ltd.

03 04 05 06 07   10 9 8 7 6 5 4 3 2 1

For a complete list of titles available from Osprey Publishing
please contact:

Osprey Direct UK, PO Box 140,
Wellingborough, Northants, NN8 2FA, UK.
Email: info@ospreydirect.co.uk

Osprey Direct USA, c/o MBI Publishing,
PO Box 1, 729 Prospect Avenue,
Osceola, WI 54020, USA.
Email: info@ospreydirectusa.com

www.ospreypublishing.com

Contents

Introduction

The Gulf War of 1991 is still one of the most fascinating military campaigns in modern memory. For seven brief months, an awesome array of American military muscle, supported by a coalition of allies, was built up in the Persian Gulf region and then unleashed in a lightning campaign that destroyed the opposition with consummate ease. This was a new type of warfare that captivated spectators by its unprecedented sophistication and firepower. New military terminology was injected into the global vocabulary, for example, 'stealth planes' and 'smart bombs', which provided a new perspective on warfare: 'weapons vision' or video imagery showing munitions hitting targets with absolute precision. It was also a media war that propelled a little-known news company, Cable Network News (CNN), into the pre-eminent position in global communications that it continues to hold today.

The impact of the Gulf War on the subject of international relations was profound. It marked the first major crisis of the new post-Cold-War period that did not stem from

The measure of Mikhail Gorbachev's greatness as a politician is testified by the peaceful collapse of the Soviet Union in contrast to the tragedy that engulfed the former Yugoslavia. (Topham Picturepoint)

President George Bush (Snr) knew all about the hazards of combat having fought against the Japanese in the Second World War. (Topham Picturepoint)

which international affairs could move away from the debilitating effects of nuclear rivalry, arms races and brinkmanship towards a more harmonious future. Academics like Francis Fukayama argued that the 'end of history' had arrived, with the world finally free of the destructive clash of competing ideologies that had dominated the 20th century with such adverse effects. Now, capitalism, supported by liberal democracy, was the only viable way forward, where political systems would rarely, if ever, be incompatible and the future would be a peaceful one.

The crisis in the Gulf region, sparked by Iraq's invasion of Kuwait in the late summer of 1990, muddied these hopeful visions of global affairs. A new bogeyman emerged in the international arena in the form of Iraqi leader, Saddam Hussein, who ordered his massive

The Gulf crisis transformed Saddam Hussein's position as a staunch ally of the west into an international pariah. (Topham Picturepoint)

the old rivalry between the United States and the Soviet Union. Indeed, the Soviet Union was by then a shadow of its former self, and its reformist leader, Mikhail Gorbachev, was struggling to hold the unwieldy and disintegrating mass together. In Europe, the Iron Curtain had fallen and the oppressed states of eastern Europe stretched out their hands towards capitalism, democracy and, in the case of Germany, unification. For the victorious United States, under the direction of George Bush (Snr), the end of bipolarity offered the world a fresh start, which he idealistically labelled the 'new world order', in

President Hosni Mubarak is one of the most influential leaders in the Middle East whose opinions carry enormous weight both regionally and internationally. (Topham Picturepoint)

region itself, neighbouring powers had hoped for an Arab solution but this never materialised. Saddam's silver-tongued diplomacy prior to the attack and then his outright lie to Egypt's president, Hosni Mubarak – that he would not invade – represented a humiliating loss of face for many in the region. In the United Nations, Iraqi aggression was openly condemned and President Bush, supported by his staunchest ally, Britain, at the time led by Margaret Thatcher, the 'Iron Lady', pushed for a more robust response. A coalition of those wishing to resolve the crisis by force, which included nations as diverse as France, Pakistan and Egypt, was slowly formed. The key question was: where could this military option be deployed in order to influence Saddam Hussein? The question was answered by satellite intelligence which showed significant numbers of Iraqi tanks moving towards Kuwait's border with Saudi Arabia. Fears about a possible occupation persuaded this most conservative of Gulf countries to

The Persian Gulf crisis was Margaret Thatcher's political swan-song – she was replaced by John Major as Prime Minister in late November 1990. (Topham Picturepoint)

armed forces to seize Iraq's rich, though weak in military terms, neighbour. Ironically, just a few years before the invasion, this subsequently demonised dictator had been a close partner of many western nations who had liberally supplied him with weapons to support his fight against the spread of Iranian fundamentalism (see Essential Histories: *The Iran–Iraq War 1980–1988*).

The critical issue that transformed the situation in the Gulf from a regional dispute into a full-blown international crisis was, above all, the substantial oil reserves in that area and the world's dependence on this 'black gold'. If left to his own devices, Saddam Hussein possessed the ability to have influence over, or outright control of, 40 per cent of the known oil supplies on the planet by combining his own reserves with Kuwait and, possibly, that of Saudi Arabia.

The international reaction to the potential Iraqi seizure of Kuwait was mixed. In the accept foreign intervention in the form of armed forces from the United States and its allies in the hope of preventing a potential loss of sovereignty.

In purely military terms, the crisis in the Gulf in 1990 came at a good time for the United States. The long Cold War had produced a massive build-up of conventional and nuclear forces, particularly based in Europe. The end of the Cold War in 1989 with the fall of the Berlin Wall appeared to offer a means of saving an enormous amount of money through cutbacks in military spending or what was commonly known as the 'peace dividend'. However, such radical ideas would

General Colin Powell was the first African American to reach the highest levels of command in the armed forces of the United States. (Topham Picturepoint)

take time to implement and, in 1990, the United States still possessed an enormous pool of military resources and personnel on which it could draw in times of crisis.

Overall command of the military operations in the Gulf region devolved from the chairman of the Joint Chiefs-of-Staff, General Colin Powell, to the part of the United States armed forces that had responsibility for this region of the world, Central Command (CENTCOM), based in Tampa, Florida and headed by the pugnacious General H. Norman Schwarzkopf. By fortunate coincidence, rudimentary plans had already been established for such a scenario and this had been played out (war-gamed) just a few weeks before the actual invasion. Two phases of operations eventually emerged from the military appreciation of the situation: firstly, Operation Desert Shield would initiate a gradual build-up of forces in Saudi Arabia; and secondly, Operation Desert Storm would mark the shift from a defensive strategy to an offensive one to eject the Iraqi forces out of Kuwait. Over 500,000 American troops, augmented by around 250,000 coalition soldiers, and thousands of main battle tanks (MBTs), combat aircraft and six-carrier battle groups were moved into the theatre of operations during this period.

Great doubts haunted the coalition forces before the battle for Kuwait. Firstly, the Iraqi armed forces were formidable (the army alone was reputed to be the fourth largest in the world) and they, unlike many of the coalition forces, had been tested in recent combat. Secondly, their leader was quite willing to sacrifice tens of thousands of his soldiers to achieve his aims. For those in the United States, the bitter memory of Vietnam hung over them like an unwelcome spectre. Critics suggested that the effect of excessive casualties would kill the campaign because American society would no longer accept such losses. Images of trench warfare that had characterised the Iran–Iraq war and, of course, the bloody stalemate of the First World War in Europe were brought back by military pundits who fed the desire of news networks for a prediction of the outcome.

The Middle East

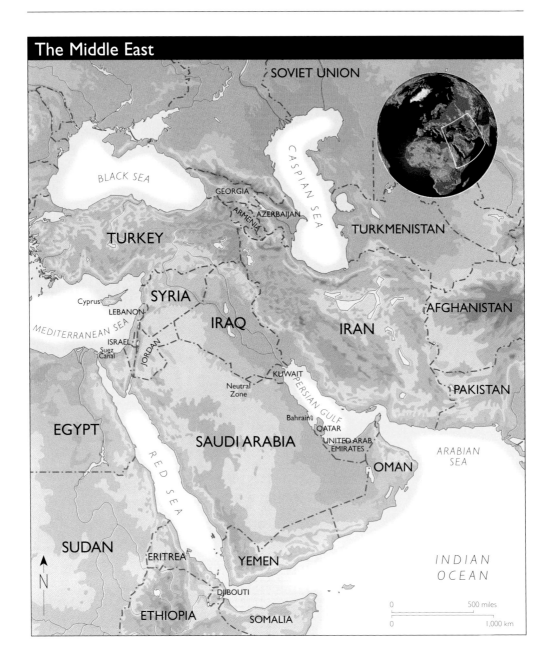

But the reality was quite different. The armed forces of the 1990s were not the same military organisations that had stumbled into the quagmire of Vietnam. Painful lessons had been learnt by the armed forces of the United States and, as the Gulf War would prove, learnt well. Technologically, the military superiority of the coalition forces was at least a generation, if not more, ahead of the opposition and that is why, after an air campaign of nearly a month, the ground campaign lasted only a matter of days. The jungle ghosts of the past were exorcised in the vast open deserts of the Middle East, and the United States demonstrated what its armed forces had known for many years, that it was, and would continue to be in the foreseeable future, militarily the most powerful nation in the world.

Chronology

1756   Autonomous Sheikdom in Kuwait under the rule of the Al-Sabah family

1913   Ottoman Empire recognises the autonomy of the Sheikh of Kuwait

1932   Iraq becomes an independent state

1958   Iraq's monarch bloodily deposed by General Abd Al-Karim Qassem

1961   **June**   Kuwait gains independence from British rule

     July   Britain provides military assistance to Kuwait against Iraqi aggression

1963   Qassem overthrown by a Ba'th party takeover

     Iraq recognises Kuwait's independence

1968   Ba'th party returns to power under Ahmad Hasan Al-Bakr and his deputy, Saddam Hussein

1979   Saddam Hussein officially takes over control of Iraq

1980   Iran–Iraq war breaks out

1988   Iran–Iraq war ends

1990   **February**   Arab Co-operation Council in Amman; Saddam demands money from Kuwait and the United Arab Emirates (UAE)

     15 July   Saddam starts moving elements of the Republican Guard to the border with Kuwait

     16 July   Iraqi foreign minister, Tariq Aziz, sets out Iraq's demands of Kuwait to the secretary-general of the Arab League, Chadly Klibi

     19 July   Kuwaiti armed forces stood down from alert; threat not taken seriously

     24 July   Saddam assures Hosni Mubarak that he will not invade Kuwait

     25 July   Saddam meets with US Ambassador April Glaspie in Baghdad and reasserts his lack of intention to invade Kuwait

     31 July   Iraqi and Kuwaiti delegates meet in Jeddah but fail to reach agreement

     2 August   Iraq invades Kuwait with over 100,000 troops and nearly 2,000 tanks; the unprepared Kuwaiti Army (16,000 in total) is overwhelmed in a matter of hours; the Royal Family flees to Saudi Arabia.

     United Nations Security Council Resolution (UNSCR) 660 condemns the Iraqi invasion and calls for an immediate withdrawal of forces

     6 August   UNSCR 661 places economic sanctions on Iraq

     7 August   US troops and aircraft – Desert Shield – start deploying to Saudi Arabia

     29 November   UNSCR 678 places a deadline of 15 January 1991 for Iraq to withdraw from Kuwait or face hostilities

1991   **16 January**   7.00 pm Washington time and 3.00 am (17 January) Iraq/Kuwait time, the Gulf War and Desert Storm begin with the coalition air campaign

     18 January   Iraqi ballistic missiles hit Israel

     29 January–1 February   Battle of Al Khafji

     24 February   The land campaign starts

     25 February   Iraqi troops start to withdraw from Kuwait

     27 February   Battle of Madinah Ridge

     28 February   Coalition ceasefire

     2 March   UNSCR 686 set out terms for the ceasefire

     3 March   Formal ceasefire agreed with Iraqi representatives

The origins of the Gulf War

The Gulf War of 1991 was a remarkable conflict in that it occurred at all. Just six months before the outbreak of hostilities, all of the parties involved in the conflict had enjoyed cordial relations based on shared ideological values (an opposition to Islamic fundamentalism) and solid trade agreements that encompassed weapons sales as well as nuclear technology. Then everything changed. The common ally became the common enemy and thousands of coalition soldiers were sent to forcibly dismember Iraq's armed forces – forces which, just a few months before, politicians of the coalition countries had helped to sustain. A new international pariah in Saddam Hussein was created virtually overnight and his existence, or survival, in 2003, is once again generating talk in the United States and abroad of a desire to remove him once and for all from power. The origins of the Gulf War are almost as absorbing as the fighting itself and demonstrate how quickly, in the shifting sands of international politics, a nation and a political leader can fall from international favour.

The role of the Iraqi President, Saddam Hussein, cannot be over-stressed in the evolution of the Gulf War. In the global political arena, he holds the dubious honour of being the most vilified leader on the planet for the last decade, which represents quite a turnaround from his status as the staunch Middle-Eastern ally in the fight against the spread of Islamic fundamentalism in the 1980s. Nobody is perhaps more surprised at this rapid decline in his international image than Saddam himself!

The root cause of his fall from grace can be traced to the disastrous war against Iran in 1980 and its economic impact on Iraq. History records (and is often retold on popular news networks) that Saddam started the war against Iran, but what is generally not mentioned is that it was Iranian

The Iranian Revolution of 1979 brought to power the Islamic fundamentalist regime of Ayatollah Khomeini at the expense of the Shah. The subsequent seizure of American diplomats in Tehran and the inability, both diplomatically and militarily, of the United States to gain their release provoked a very hostile western response to the Iranian Revolution. The widespread publicity of the burnt bodies of the US servicemen in the botched Operation Eagle Claw in 1980 added to America's hatred of this new regime and fundamentally undermined President Carter's administration. In addition, the willingness of Iran to sponsor uprisings in neighbouring countries, particularly among Shi'ite communities, has since led to unrest in Bahrain, Iraq, Kuwait and Saudi Arabia. (Topham Picturepoint)

provocation that led to the hostilities and that the Iraqi president ordered a very limited incursion into Iranian territory to send a political message to the Iranians to keep out of Iraqi domestic affairs. War, however, is a difficult phenomenon to control (especially when the other side wants to keep fighting) and the conflict escalated for another eight years despite Saddam's attempts to end it quickly. The war against Iran transformed Iraq from a rich and prosperous country into a pauper. In 1980, Iraq possessed over $30 billion in foreign-exchange reserves, but by 1988, it owed nearly $100 billion to overseas creditors and the cost of repairing the war damage to the country's infrastructure was estimated to be more than twice that amount. Iraq's major source of foreign revenue was generated by oil reserves, but by the end of the Iran–Iraq War, Iraq was earning just over $10 billion a year from these sales due primarily to the glut of oil in international markets and the subsequent low prices.

In political terms, the state of Iraq's economic woes directly threatened the well-being of the President himself. Saddam's rise to power had been characterised by brutal and ruthless policies towards friends and enemies alike. Most famously, Saddam had used even the most internationally unacceptable methods to repress his foes – that of chemical weapons against his own Kurdish population as well as against Iranian soldiers. Violence had been a significant part of Iraqi politics since the end of the Second World War and two of Saddam's predecessors met painful deaths while in office, notably the Iraqi Regent in 1958 who was torn to pieces by an angry mob, and his successor, General Qassem, who was gunned down in 1963. It is still highly possible that Saddam will meet his end in a similar way. Adding to his troubles, he possessed thousands of fit, young men who had been trained to kill and who now wanted to be fully demobilised. With the poor state of the Iraqi economy, Saddam could not let them out onto the streets to face unemployment. This was a similar

dilemma to that faced by the British Government after the First World War and which led to the creation of unemployment benefit, but Saddam was simply not in a financial position to offer this societal release-valve. Iraq needed a rapid injection of capital if Saddam's regime was to survive. The question was: where would it come from?

Iraq's relationship with the wider world had generally been very good until 1990. In the United States, Saddam found an important partner. The old adage 'the enemy of my enemy is my friend' perhaps sums up the relationship between the United States and Iraq in the 1980s. The loss of a friendly Iranian regime and the humiliating failure of Operation Eagle Claw (the Special Forces attempt to rescue US diplomats) encouraged the United States to support an equally undesirable regime. The key area of trade concerned economic credits, providing much-needed food, but some weapons arrived by means of unofficial channels through neighbouring countries. This relationship, though, suffered some setbacks, particularly the mistaken attack on the USS *Stark* by an Iraqi warplane firing Exocet missiles which killed 37 sailors in 1987; and, by 1990, the Bush administration had serious doubts as to whether the agricultural

The further development of Iraq's nuclear capability, based on a small French nuclear reactor, alarmed several of Iraq's neighbours, most notably Iran and Israel. Iran attacked the fledgling facilities in 1980 with a small air strike that caused little damage. Israel, however, initiated Operation Babylon on 7 June 1981, a large air strike by eight F-16 fighter bombers using 2,000 lb bombs with six F-15s acting as top cover, on Iraq's nuclear-weapons plant at Osirak and completely destroyed it. This attack retarded the development of Saddam Hussein's nuclear weapons programme by several years.

credits were being used to help the Iraqi population or to support the Iraqi military machine. Nevertheless, annual trade between the United States and Iraq amounted to just over $3 billion by 1990.

In Europe, Saddam Hussein found many willing partners who were not as circumspect as the United States with regard to weapons sales. France, in particular, developed a fruitful relationship that amounted to sales of arms worth billions of francs by the end of the 1980s. In addition, it was France who supplied Iraq with the technology to build another nuclear reactor from the late 1970s onwards (the first one had been supplied by the USSR in 1968). The only impediment to further sales concerned justifiable doubts

One of the most interesting consequences of the new restrictions on weapons sales to Iraq was the seizure of British-made parts for the 'Super Gun' project. The 'Super Gun' was based on an old idea (derived from the huge German cannon that bombarded Paris in the First World War) that a very large artillery gun could fire a projectile extremely long distances, that is, over hundreds of miles. Such a weapon could be fitted with a variety of warheads (conventional, chemical, biological and/or nuclear) and would be a dangerous regional threat to all of Iraq's neighbours. The inventor of the new gun was the brilliant Canadian scientist Dr Gerald Bull who had a great deal of experience in designing relatively compact artillery guns to hit targets at very long distances. The project failed because the British Government embargoed the parts and Dr Bull was mysteriously assassinated in Brussels in 1990. The successful development of this weapon would have dramatically altered the military balance in the region and fundamentally challenged traditional ideas about the importance of air-power and ballistic missiles in modern warfare.

raised at the end of the 1980s as to whether Iraq could afford to purchase more weapons, as the credit debt to France alone was growing rapidly. Britain also developed a significant amount of trade with Iraq and was its third largest trading partner by 1990. However, increasing concerns about Saddam's human-rights record, reinforced by the execution of Farzad Bazoft, a journalist working for the *Observer* in 1990, generated enormous pressure to halt arms sales to Iraq. Beyond western Europe, the bulk of Iraq's military capability was drawn from its good relationship with the Soviet Union but that, too, with the rise to power of Mikhail Gorbachev, now faced an uncertain future. Gorbachev, unlike previous leaders of the Soviet Union, took a more balanced approach to Middle-Eastern affairs, rather than just openly supporting the Arab side. Furthermore, his attention was focused more on addressing the huge financial problems facing the crumbling Soviet Union which weighed more heavily on his foreign-policy agenda than Saddam's cash crisis.

From the regional perspective, Saddam's links with his neighbours, Saudi Arabia, Kuwait, the UAE and, to a lesser extent, Egypt and Syria, had grown weaker since the reduction of the common threat from Iran with the ending of the Iran–Iraq War. His closest allies, Jordan and the stateless Palestine Liberation Organisation (PLO), were hardly in a position to help financially. Aid from Israel was simply not an option given the traditional enmity between the two states. Iraq had borrowed heavily from its richer neighbours in the Gulf. Now the issue of war-debt repayment (measured in tens of billions of dollars) was high on the diplomatic agenda with these nations. Yet Iraq was unable to pay back the debt and in fact needed a rapid transfusion of money that these states were unwilling to provide. The other sticking point with these nations concerned the failure to meet the strict Organisation of Petroleum Exporting Countries (OPEC) quotas for oil output. More oil on the international market meant lower prices per barrel, further reducing Iraq's ability to resolve its financial problems. OPEC had called for a limit of 22 million barrels a day but by 1990 oil production had already exceeded that figure by approximately two million barrels and the price of oil had dipped to $18 a barrel by the spring of 1990. The major culprits in this deliberate overproduction were Kuwait and the UAE whose strategy was to deliberately drive down the price of oil so that more nations became dependent on OPEC oil. In

By the 1980s, OPEC was a shadow of its former self compared to its positions in the 1970s. At one time, it appeared to hold the developed nations to ransom over their dependency on oil and could use that as a powerful political tool. However, its policies of generating high prices by restricting the flow of oil backfired in the medium term because western nations were forced to turn to alternative sources of supply. As a consequence, OPEC countries had lost a significant proportion of the oil market and now, quite logically, many of the Gulf states realised that, to recapture the market, oil output must go up and prices must go down to encourage more nations to return to the traditional suppliers of petroleum.

the long term, all would benefit as the prices would inevitably rise, but in the short term, such a strategy placed even greater pressure on the fragile Iraqi economy.

In sum, the financial crisis in Iraq had reached breaking point by early 1990 and Saddam Hussein was in a desperate position. One immediate sign of the growing catastrophe in Iraqi politics was the resurgence of violence towards the leader. In personal terms, since 1988, the president had experienced four assassination attempts (one from his élite Republican Guard), clearly a manifestation of growing discontent with his rule. The pressure had to be relieved somehow but traditional avenues of financial aid either through western support, the Soviet Union or neighbouring countries were drying up rapidly. Saddam had alienated the west through his appalling human-rights record, the USSR was in financial crisis, and the militarily weak but very wealthy regional nations were indifferent to his plight. Time was running out for Saddam and the only card left in his hand, given the dwindling price of oil, bore the emblem of the Iraqi armed forces that still remained a powerful force. Nevertheless, to any outside observer in 1990, the short-term career of Saddam Hussein, like many of the former dictators in communist-dominated eastern Europe, looked distinctly limited.

Iraq and the coalition forces

The Iraqi armed forces

On paper, Iraq possessed impressive military forces that had experienced eight years of conflict just two years prior to the outbreak of the Gulf War. The Iraqi Army alone was reputed to be the fourth largest in the world, with approximately one million men under arms, a number that could be doubled with full conscription of men aged 18–34. In terms of equipment, its 60-odd divisions were equipped with nearly 6,000 MBTs ranging from the venerable T-55 through to the much-respected T-72. At the infantryman level, the standard small arm was the Kalashnikov AK-47 which was more than a match for any other rifle in existence and many of these soldiers, especially those in the élite Republican Guard had years of combat experience behind them. In close support of these soldiers were almost 200 armed helicopters, including the powerful Mi-24 Hind gunship that had performed so well against guerrilla forces in Afghanistan. Iraq's air-defence network was one of the most comprehensive in the world with around 10,000 anti-aircraft guns (AAA),

The T-72 MBT was a dangerous threat to coalition tanks. (TRH Pictures)

ABOVE The AK-47 is arguably the most successful small arm of the post-war period. Produced in the Soviet Union by Mikhail Kalashnikov since 1947, it has been the weapon of choice for many armies throughout the world. The success of the gun lies with its simple and rugged design that allows even the most inexperienced soldier (from the age of 10 upwards in some countries) to be able to handle the weapon effectively. Unlike many of the highly sophisticated yet often environmentally sensitive rifles produced in the west, the AK-47 is a very reliable performer under most conditions and will continue to be a popular weapon for the foreseeable future. (Public domain)

RIGHT AM-39 Exocet. (TRH Pictures)

The Republican Guard was Saddam Hussein's personal bodyguard unit. It was equipped with the best troops and the latest military equipment not only to fight the external enemies of Iraq but also to suppress internal dissent as well. It is estimated that Saddam had 12 Republican Guard divisions by 1990 and they represented the most serious threat to the coalition forces on the ground.

16,000 surface-to-air missiles (SAMs) such as the Soviet SA-2, (as well as the entire family of subsequently developed missiles up to the SA-16) and the Franco-German Roland missiles.

In the air, the Iraqi Air Force (the sixth largest in the world) also appeared highly capable, with over 900 planes of various types. Saddam Hussein had equipped his air force with aircraft from a range of countries, though most came from the Soviet Union. His stockpile of aircraft acquired from the USSR included the MiG-21, MiG-23, MiG-25, and the much-feared Mig-29 Fulcrum as well as the Su-7, Su-20, Su-22, Su-24, and the highly capable Su-25 Frogfoot ground-attack aircraft. His arsenal also included bombers like the Tupolev Tu-16 and Tu-22 as well as the impressive French Mirage F-1 high-performance fighter-bombers. In terms of weaponry for air combat, the Iraqi Air Force boasted Soviet AA-2, AA-6, AA-7, AA-8 as well as French-made R-550 Magic air-to-air missiles. For attack against land or sea targets, its most sophisticated missiles and bombs were predominantly obtained from France; for example, the AS-30L laser-guided bomb (LGB) and the deadly air-launched AM-39 Exocet anti-ship missiles which proved to be so dangerous in the Falklands War of 1982 (see Essential Histories: *The Falklands War 1982*). Adding to this impressive demonstration of firepower, Iraq had invested heavily in the infrastructure of the air force from the construction of 50 significant bases with good runways to hardened aircraft shelters and an integrated command, control and communications (C3) network.

The smallest component of the Iraqi armed forces was its navy, hardly surprising given the small amount of coastline to which the country has access, yet this force still packed significant punch. In theory, Iraq had 165 naval vessels at its disposal but the bulk of them were obsolete; however, it did possess seven Osa warships armed with Styx anti-ship missiles. This enormous missile had a range of 16–45 miles (25–72 km) with a 1,100 lb warhead and became famous when Egyptian missile boats using it sank the Israeli destroyer, *Eilat*, in 1967. To many observers, the Styx missile heralded a new age of naval warfare in which the missile and not the capital ship would dominate the future theatre of operations. Iraq also possessed about 50 land-based Chinese derivatives of this missile called the Silkworm which had a range of around 70 miles (112 km) and travelled at roughly the same speed as the Styx, around Mach 0.9. In addition, the Iraqi Navy had a number of small patrol boats, a few ex-Soviet landing ships and mine-warfare vessels. Even more worrying perhaps than these conventional forces were Iraq's chemical, biological and fledgling nuclear weapons. It was known that Saddam had developed 2,000–4,000 tons of mustard gas

Mustard gas was first introduced into modern warfare during the First World War. It is a blistering agent that causes extreme pain on contact and can have fatal effects. The blisters caused by this gas take a long time to heal. Sarin and Tabun are nerve agents that interfere with the nervous system producing muscular spasms and paralysis. Like mustard gas, their effects can be fatal. Botulinum is a biological toxin that produces symptoms including a dry mouth, visual impairment, speech problems, dizziness and vomiting. These toxins are highly dangerous and death from respiratory failure often occurs within hours.

and nerve agents like Sarin and Tabun. Western intelligence agencies also suspected that Iraq was developing biological weapons like botulinum and typhoid bacteria. Furthermore, Saddam utilised delivery vehicles in the form of approximately 800 Scud-B (surface-to-surface) missiles and several hundred home-grown versions like the Al-Husayn that could hit Israel and Saudi Arabia with ease. All in all, the Iraqi military machine represented one of the most potent armed forces in the entire region.

The coalition forces

It has been estimated that coalition forces totalled just under 800,000 troops at the height of the Gulf War, with over half a million being provided by the United States. This injection of military manpower was very important given that Iraq's immediate neighbours, Kuwait (subsequently occupied) and Saudi Arabia had less than 60,000 regular troops between them – a force clearly dwarfed by the Iraqi military machine. The United States not only provided the bulk of the manpower in the Gulf War but also the majority of the military hardware in the air, on land and at sea to bring about a victorious conclusion to the military campaign. In the air campaign, the United States and its allies deployed the most sophisticated aerial-weapons systems in human history. The air assets drew on a pool of approximately 2,000 combat aircraft that ranged from the futuristic looking F-117A stealth fighter to the more conventional F-15s, F-16s and the British Tornado. Furthermore, the US Air Force even turned to its aged B-52 bomber (designed in the 1950s) to deploy air-launched cruise missiles (ALCMs). A wide variety of aircraft was utilised over the skies of Iraq, from the more glamorous strike aircraft to the little-talked-about electronic warfare assets like the EF-111A Ravens, the vital E-3A airborne warning and control system (AWACS) and the hundreds of critical aerial tankers, for example, the KC-135 Stratotankers, which allowed the attacks to take place deep within

ABOVE The Lockheed F-117A stealth fighter entered service with the US Air Force in 1983. This futuristic black, bat-shaped aircraft was a response to the horrendous losses endured by US warplanes over Vietnam to ground-based SAM networks that targeted aircraft by using powerful radars. (Missiles are either radar- or infrared- (IR) guided and lock on to the hot exhaust of an aeroplane). The F-117A was designed from the outset to minimise the radar and heat 'signature' of the aircraft by clever use of radar-absorbing material and the special shape of the plane as well as by masking as much as possible the heat exhausts. It proved to be spectacularly successful in the Gulf War. (US Air Force)

BELOW The F-16 Fighting Falcon. (US Air Force)

enemy territory. Likewise, the armada of transport aircraft from the gigantic C-5B Galaxy to the ubiquitous C-130 Hercules enabled the United States and coalition forces to transport vast amounts of personnel and equipment to the Gulf region in a remarkably short period.

On land, the ground units facing the Iraqi forces were some of the most powerful in history in terms of firepower. The US Army of the 1990s was a quantum leap ahead of the army of the Vietnam era. Firstly, it was an all-volunteer army supported by huge numbers of willing reservists. Secondly, in terms of equipment, it was a vastly more sophisticated force. The standard tank was the M1 Abrams

MIAI MBT. The M1 Abrams was introduced in the 1980s to replace the old M60A3 MBT and, by 1990, four versions existed: the M1, the IPM1 (improved armour), the MIA1 (a new 120 mm gun instead of the standard 105 mm) and the MIA1HA (heavy armour) with uranium armour which is claimed to be almost impenetrable. Initially, M1s were deployed in Desert Shield but 90 per cent were replaced by the more powerful MIA1 and MIA1HA before the ground offensive was initiated. (TRH Pictures)

and later M1A1 (improved version) that added combined speed and firepower to a comprehensive and reliable package. A proportion of the mechanised infantry that worked in concert with the heavy armour also used the relatively new Bradley fighting vehicle (M2IFV and M3CFV) with its powerful 25 mm chain gun and two TOW (tube-launched optically tracked wire-guided) anti-tank missiles. The basic rifle was the M-16A2, a perfected version of an earlier model that had proved susceptible to the dust of south-east Asia and in Vietnam had developed a nasty habit of jamming at critical moments. The new rifle, however, was less prone to jamming, packed a longer-range capability and, if kept clean, performed well. The sophistication of the artillery deployed to the Gulf was impressive from the multiple-launch rocket systems (MLRS) to the standard 155 mm M109 self-propelled Howitzer. The firepower of the MLRS was at least a generation ahead of that of the Iraqi opposition. In support of these armoured formations, the US Army fielded sizeable numbers of battlefield helicopters from the aggressive Apache and Cobra to the

Key coalition airbases, supply routes and supporting carrier battle forces

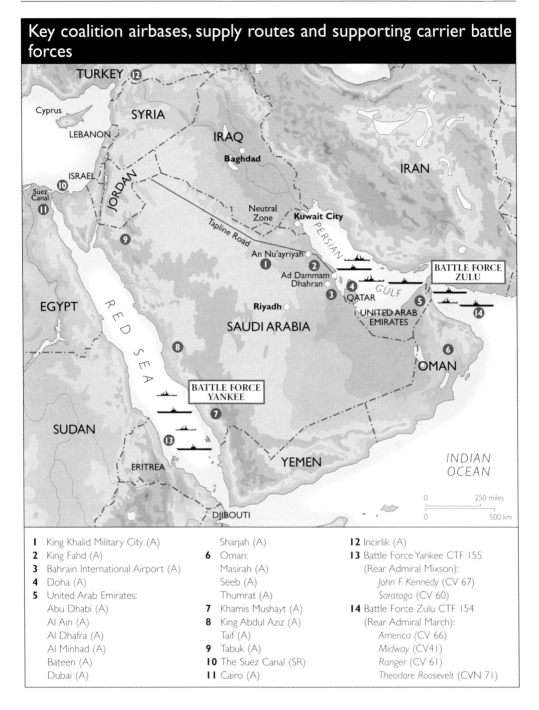

1	King Khalid Military City (A)	Sharjah (A)	12 Incirlik (A)
2	King Fahd (A)	6 Oman:	13 Battle Force Yankee CTF 155
3	Bahrain International Airport (A)	Masirah (A)	(Rear Admiral Mixson):
4	Doha (A)	Seeb (A)	*John F Kennedy* (CV 67)
5	United Arab Emirates:	Thumrat (A)	*Saratoga* (CV 60)
	Abu Dhabi (A)	7 Khamis Mushayt (A)	14 Battle Force Zulu CTF 154
	Al Ain (A)	8 King Abdul Aziz (A)	(Rear Admiral March):
	Al Dhafra (A)	Taif (A)	*America* (CV 66)
	Al Minhad (A)	9 Tabuk (A)	*Midway* (CV41)
	Bateen (A)	10 The Suez Canal (SR)	*Ranger* (CV 61)
	Dubai (A)	11 Cairo (A)	*Theodore Roosevelt* (CVN 71)

Black Hawk and Huey support helicopters. These capabilities offered enormous flexibility, rapid movement and devastating firepower.

The US Navy along with coalition forces provided the seaborne punch to the campaign against Iraq and its commitment grew steadily to six-carrier battle groups. The sheer size of a US Navy aircraft-carrier provided a floating strike platform for over 70 aircraft that included the F-14 Tomcat (made famous by the popular film, *Top Gun*), F/A-18 Hornets, A-7 Corsairs, A-6 Intruders and supporting helicopters. Amphibious assault ships like the LHA 4 Nassau provided a base for thousands of US Marine Corps combat soldiers and their unique AV-8 Harrier jump jets. Aegis class cruisers and even the Second-World-War renovated battleships like the USS *Missouri* were sent to the Gulf region now bristling with state-of-the-art equipment and carrying the powerful Tomahawk land-attack missiles (TLAMs). All of these major surface units were surrounded by a host of smaller ships such as frigates to provide close protection to these very valuable assets. The naval commitment to the Gulf War was an important component of the overall strategy to liberate Kuwait and all of the heavy armour and the main part of the logistical support for these forces had to be transported by sea. Air power simply could not carry the bulk items like armour and ammunition in the quantities required by the land forces, but sea power could do it by using the tremendous lifting capacity of modern shipping. Overall, the coalition forces accrued a staggering amount of disposable firepower (the bulk of it from the United States) and would demonstrate its effectiveness with the outbreak of hostilities in mid-January 1991.

The AH-64 Apache helicopter is one of the most powerful battlefield helicopters in the world. It was normally armed with eight laser-guided Hellfire missiles (with a range of around 4 miles (7 km)), 38 Hydra 2.75-inch rockets and 1,200 rounds of 30 mm cannon ammunition during the Gulf War. (TRH Pictures)

Saddam invades Kuwait

By spring 1990, Saddam Hussein was desperately seeking a financial solution to his rapidly downward-spiralling economic and political situation. In February of that year at the Arab Co-operation Council in Jordan, the Iraqi leader put forward the idea of a suspension of his country's wartime debts and the urgent need for extra funding, but his pleas fell on deaf ears among his Arab neighbours. Furthermore, his continual requests for oil quotas to be adhered to in order to halt the slide in the price of oil were also ignored. In fact, the attitude of both Kuwait and the UAE to his calls for a cancellation of wartime debts and more credit were decidedly unhelpful: no debt would be absolved and the only money that Iraq would receive from them would be in the form of charity. This blunt rebuff of Saddam Hussein generated a very dangerous condition for an Arab leader (often underestimated by western politicians) – that of a humiliating loss of face. The collapse of Saddam's dignity combined with the perilous state of the Iraqi economy brought about a sharp contrast in policy by the summer of 1990.

At the height of July, Iraq adopted a dual-track policy of intense diplomacy allied with military manoeuvres near the border with Kuwait. The diplomatic line consisted of a series of accusations of Kuwait: firstly, that it had stolen oil from Iraq's Rumaila oilfield (near the Iraq–Kuwait border), estimated to be over $2 billion in value, which should be immediately repaid; secondly, that its loans to Iraq in the 1980s were largely from oil profits due to overproduction (exceeding OPEC quotas), which was harming its neighbour; and thirdly, that Kuwait had a long-held secret agenda to acquire Iraqi territory while Iraq was distracted by the fight against Islamic fundamentalism. The proposed Iraqi solution to these crimes

encompassed a huge cash rebate, a price hike in oil prices to at least $25 a barrel, the complete suspension of war debts and a comprehensive financial package to aid the economic reconstruction of Iraq. To support his diplomacy, Saddam concurrently started moving large numbers of the élite Republican Guard towards the border with Kuwait, with just under 40,000 troops in position by the 19 July.

The Kuwaiti reaction, after the initial shock of Iraq's new hard-line policies, was surprising. Having digested all of the diplomatic and military information, the Kuwaiti political administration came to the staggering conclusion that Saddam was not serious and was just trying to improve his negotiating position. On 19 July, despite having initially been put on alert, the Kuwaiti armed forces were stood down just as the Iraqi forces were building up along the border. At this point in the growing crisis, it was conceivable that, perhaps with a more flexible attitude on the part of the Kuwaitis, the invasion could have been averted. However, the subsequent diplomatic response ensured that a collision course was set. The official Kuwaiti line was bullish in a letter to the secretary-general of the Arab League, Chadly Klibi, and categorically denied Iraq's accusations, stating that Kuwait would not surrender to threats. The reaction of the Arab League itself was to send Egypt's president, Hosni Mubarak, to act as mediator between the two sides and to try to generate a peaceful resolution of the crisis.

Mubarak's mission came away from Baghdad with the impression from Saddam himself that Iraq would not invade Kuwait and was willing to start face-to-face negotiations at a summit in Jeddah in the Kingdom of Saudi Arabia on 31 July. The peaceful tone set by Mubarak's impression of

Saddam's intentions was further reinforced by his meeting with the US Ambassador to Iraq, April Glaspie, on 25 July. The United States had been worried about Saddam's new approach to negotiations with Kuwait, in particular the build-up of military forces that was clearly identified through intelligence assets in the region. The choice of a female ambassador to a Muslim country in which gender equality was certainly not regarded in the same way as in the United States raises certain questions in retrospect. Did Saddam see beyond Glaspie's gender and take her seriously, or, instead, did her gender reduce the weight of her message? In this meeting, Glaspie stressed that the border dispute should be resolved peacefully, but at no stage did she convey any threat to Saddam about the consequences of force being used. This fact has led historians to question whether the United States inadvertently gave Saddam a green light or merely failed to show a red one. In fact, Glaspie came away from the meeting so reassured and with a pledge from Saddam not to invade Kuwait that she felt happy to go back to Washington (and a long-planned holiday) on 30 July. To the west, all signs pointed towards peace, despite the fact that over 100,000 Iraqi troops were on the border with Kuwait.

The end game of Iraq's diplomacy was played out in the evening of 31 July in Jeddah when Saddam's representative, Izzat Ibrahim, the Vice-President of Iraq's Revolutionary Command Council, started talks with the Kuwaiti Crown Prince, Sa'd Abdallah Al-Sabah. Iraq brought to the table a demand for $10 billion for the loss of oil from the Rumaila oilfields in exchange for which the massive army on the border with Kuwait would be substantially reduced. The Kuwaitis offered $9 billion in order to score a diplomatic point: Saddam would not get everything he demanded. Again, personal honour was at stake, and the Kuwaiti brinkmanship backfired badly. With the failure to obtain Iraq's demands in full, despite an agreement to resume negotiations on the 4 August, Saddam Hussein ordered his forces to attack Kuwait. At 1.00 am,

2 August 1990, over 100,000 Iraqi soldiers with almost 2,000 tanks launched an attack on Kuwait. The invasion plan was competent and effective. The Republican Guard led the attack on Kuwait City in concert with a Special Forces division. Elsewhere in Kuwait, helicopters landed troops at strategic sites. Within 12 hours, the bulk of the resistance had been extinguished and the royal family had fled to Saudi Arabia. Kuwait's political miscalculation had proved to be nothing short of disastrous, despite some heroic fighting from elements of the Kuwaiti armed

Kuwait City.
(TRH Pictures)

forces, and now Kuwait and all its wealth belonged to Saddam Hussein.

The international reaction was one of complete surprise. All indicators had previously pointed towards a peaceful conclusion. However, now Iraqi tanks occupied Kuwait City. Regionally, many leaders had hoped for an Arab solution to an Arab problem but it simply did not appear. Saddam's unwillingness to negotiate with the Al-Sabah family in exile and the fact that many powerful Arab leaders like Hosni Mubarak had the proverbial 'egg on their faces' for telling the world that Iraq would not invade Kuwait meant that a local diplomatic solution (despite intense efforts) was unlikely. Internationally, reaction was mixed. President Bush was initially cautious about possible responses; however, his support for a military option was considerably bolstered by the intervention of Britain's Margaret Thatcher who wanted a tough response.

Traditionally, the British had always maintained a strong interest in the affairs of the Gulf states and in 1961 had guaranteed Kuwait's sovereignty against Iraqi aggression with military forces. In the United Nations (UN), reaction to Iraq's invasion was swift and the United Nations Security Council passed Resolution 660 (UNSCR) just hours after the start of hostilities, condemning the military assault and calling for an immediate withdrawal. The UN would pass a series of resolutions over the coming months that put in place an economic embargo of Iraq (UNSCR 661) and then facilitated the legitimate use of force for the coalition forces with a deadline for Iraqi withdrawal (UNSCR 678) set for the 15 January 1991.

Diplomacy with Iraq over the issue of the invasion of Kuwait was by no means a clear-cut proposition for the international community. Many nations, for example, the Soviet Union and Japan, had strong economic links with Iraq that would inevitably be damaged by heavy-handed international diplomacy. All agreed that the occupation of Kuwait was wrong, but the means to liberate the country was still an issue of debate. The United States took the lead concerning the response to Iraqi aggression. Weighing heavily on the minds of the President's advisers was the unchallengeable economic dimension: Saddam now directly controlled 20 per cent of the world's oil supplies and threatened another 20 per cent in Saudi Arabia. Diplomacy seemed unlikely to work given Saddam's intransigence towards giving up Kuwait so a greater emphasis was placed on the military angle. Remarkably, on turning to his military planners who had for years focused their attention on the Cold War, a plan existed in CENTCOM called Plan 1002-90 which was designed for just such a contingency – defending the oilfields of Saudi Arabia. The key factor would be to persuade the very conservative Islamic kingdom to accept large numbers of Christian soldiers into a country that possessed the holiest site in the

Muslim world, Mecca. A high-level delegation comprising the Secretary of Defence, Dick Cheney, the commander of CENTCOM, General Schwarzkopf, and the Deputy Adviser on National Security Affairs, Robert Gates, showed King Fahd the latest satellite intelligence that revealed thousands of Iraqi troops close to the border with Saudi Arabia on 6 August. The issue of whether Saddam intended at the time to invade Saudi Arabia is still a matter of conjecture and debate but the information that the Americans showed to the Saudis on 6 August led to an immediate decision by the King to allow the United States to move at least a quarter of a million troops to Saudi Arabia in an operation called Desert Shield.

The sheer size of the Iraqi forces in Kuwait meant that, as Plan 1002-90 had foreseen, it would take months to build up the necessary forces in order to compete on level terms. Everything needed for the future battle – tanks, aircraft, warships and, of course, critically, the soldiers – would have to be sent to the Middle East. As the US and coalition forces established themselves, the plan was modified substantially because, after all, its strategy had been to defend Saudi Arabia, rather than liberate Kuwait. Manpower levels would be tripled and coalition forces would comprise a variety of nations that included regional powers like Egypt and Syria. At the conceptual level, the idea that Christian and Muslim soldiers would fight side by side in Islam's holiest country was a scenario that few could have predicted prior to 1990. Logistics were the essence of the forthcoming war and millions of tons of military equipment were shipped out to Saudi Arabia to create one of the most powerful conventional forces in history. In the background to these preparations, intense negotiations continued, but the failure to reach agreement before the deadline for hostilities on 15 January provided a timetable for the shift from diplomacy to the use of force. The failure of Saddam to evacuate Iraqi forces from Kuwait by the stroke of midnight (GMT) 15 January 1991 led to the execution of one of the most technologically sophisticated military campaigns in human history: Operation Desert Storm.

King Fahd of Saudi Arabia faced one of the most difficult decisions of his reign when he deliberated over allowing the coalition forces into his kingdom. (Topham Picturepoint)

Operation Desert Storm

The air war

Air power dominated the media images of the Gulf War. Video footage of precision-guided munitions hitting their targets with pinpoint accuracy remains embedded in popular memory. It was, however, a very limited campaign in comparison to previous wars. The total weight of bombs dropped on Iraqi targets was just below 90,000 tons, which equates to less than two months of bombing in the Second World War or the Vietnam War, yet historians can claim with confidence that the Gulf War used air power more effectively. The key difference between the wars of 1941, 1971 and 1991 was the qualitative superiority of modern aircraft in terms of accuracy. In stark terms, a fighter-bomber of the 1990s armed with just two smart bombs possessed such a level of accuracy that it would have taken more than 100 B-17 bombers to achieve the same results.

Planning the air offensive

Coalition combat aircraft used in the air offensive were drawn from a number of countries that included Britain, Bahrain, Canada, France, Italy, Kuwait, Qatar, Saudi Arabia, the UAE and the United States. The United States, though, provided the bulk of the forces and dropped the majority of the ordinance – both precision and 'dumb' (unguided) bombs. A wide range of aircraft was deployed in the theatre and this variety provided air war planners with a number of options. The domination of enemy air space was considered to be difficult to achieve because Iraq's air-defence network was far superior to that in operation over North Vietnam during Operations Linebacker I and II and to those in existence in eastern Europe

during the Cold War. The responsibility for planning the air campaign fell to the air component of CENTCOM in the form of the 9th Air Force under the command of Lieutenant-General Charles A. Horner, based

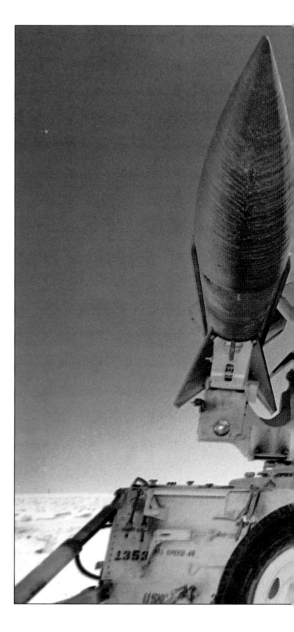

at Shaw Air Force Base, South Carolina. By devolving the air campaign to the US Air Force, this very powerful armed service could draw on all of its planning assets to formulate a comprehensive bombing strategy. One such asset was Colonel John A. Warden III of the Air Staff Plans Directorate who, with a team of officers, in a room in the Pentagon called Checkmate, began putting together a plan. The plan that emerged was 'Instant Thunder', a name that immediately conveys a contrast with 'Rolling Thunder', the much-maligned

long-term 1960s Vietnam bombing strategy. In essence, Instant Thunder was an offensive air campaign that would be short yet decisive in effect and, with some modifications, it became the blueprint for the subsequent air campaign.

These American manufactured, radar-guided Hawk surface-to-air missiles were a reliable and combat proven weapons system that put up sturdy resistance to the Iraqi invasion before eventually being overwhelmed in Kuwait. The United States deployed them in significant numbers to Saudi Arabia during Operation Desert Shield. (Topham Picturepoint)

Battlefield helicopters play a vital role in modern warfare. Large troop-carrying helicopters allow commanders to move forces in a theatre of operations with speed and precision. The biggest problem for helicopters in the Gulf War concerned sand ingestion that reduced the life of the engines dramatically. Sand filters and high-maintenance cycles were essential to keep the helicopters operational. (Topham Picturepoint)

From the mid-1970s, military thinking in the United States about air power emphasised joint operations with land forces and the integrated battlefield that linked the air campaign with the ground/sea campaign. One consequence of this new thinking was the sacking of the Air Force Chief-of-Staff,

General Michael J. Dugan, on 17 September 1990. His remarks to journalists while visiting Saudi Arabia were interpreted as suggesting that air power alone (old ideas about air doctrine) could resolve the Gulf issue. Secretary of Defence Dick Cheney fired him because his comments were out of step with the new era of jointness which perhaps indicates the level of sensitivity surrounding the issue.

Having a co-ordinated strategic plan is important in warfare, but translating this into practice is quite another process. In order to make the conceptual Instant Thunder into an actual application of air

dividing the Kuwaiti theatre of operations into 33 square boxes (with each side 30 miles (48 km) in distance) allowed planners to accurately allocate specific portions of air space to groups of attacking aircraft. Every aspect of the air campaign had to be managed, from the point of take-off, through to the bombing run and the recovery, and then repeated on a daily basis.

The weakness of Iraqi air power

In contrast to this modern approach to air warfare, the Iraqi Air Force adopted an unfashionable and fatally passive defensive strategy. To a degree, this probably reflected the poor performance of this wing of the Iraqi military machine in the Iran–Iraq War during which its aircraft suffered significant casualties while trying to carry out strategic bombing attacks. After these losses, the Iraqi Air Force took a less offensive role in the war and it is possible that the defensive posture became institutionalised. Undoubtedly, the failure to seize the strategic initiative from the coalition forces by attacking Saudi Arabia during the early phases of Desert Shield was an enormous error on the part of Saddam Hussein. His air force was well equipped with high-performance aircraft like MiG-29 Fulcrums and Mirage F1 fighter-bombers but fortunately for the coalition, the Iraqi Air Force confined itself to patrolling its own air space. Perhaps another source of this strategic complacency resided in the formidable air-defence network that Iraq possessed in 1990. The years of war against Iran had allowed Saddam to acquire state-of-the-art passive and active air defences. Iraqi radars, SAMs and AAA were well integrated and indeed Iraq boasted underground fibre-optic communications lines. The Iraqi Air Force's shelters for its aircraft were some of the strongest in the world and covered by thick reinforced concrete. Saddam's strategy predicated itself on his own ability and that of the Iraqi Air Force to weather the coming battles and inflict unacceptable casualties on the attacking forces.

power required another planning unit to match assets to targets. This new operational planning cell was placed in theatre in Riyadh under the command of Brigadier-General Buster C Glosson and became popularly known as the 'Black Hole'. It was the task of this secretive and extremely vital group of planners to produce the critical air tasking order (ATO) – the schedule that matched assets to targets within a coherent timetable. Without the ATO, attacking Iraq would be a series of uncoordinated strikes that would be a wasteful use of assets with no aim apart from hitting the enemy. The creation of 'kill boxes' after the air campaign had started,

The application of air power

The air strategy to neutralise Iraq coalesced into three distinct phases of operations that were designed to destroy the cohesion of the enemy forces and shape the battlefield for the subsequent attack by the coalition land forces. Phase 1 was aimed primarily at strategic targets from sites of weapons of mass destruction to the essential command centres. The focus of these attacks was to destroy or disrupt the centres of gravity around which revolved the Iraqi armed forces' command, control, communications and intelligence (C3I). Phase 2 targeted the air-defence network in Kuwait that would become the focus of the main theatre of operations. Air superiority over the battlefield, as history has demonstrated time and time again, is an essential component of victory on the ground. Phase 3 shifted the aerial attacks to the Iraqi ground units in Kuwait. These forces would be subjected to precision attacks and carpet-bombing, both day and night, that would psychologically as well as physically degrade the ability of the Iraqis to put up effective resistance to the coalition land assault. The rapid success of the air war meant that the idea of attacking targets in each phase of operations sequentially over a fixed period was quickly set aside and replaced by simultaneous strikes at every level, thus increasing the tempo of the overall strategy.

Task Force Normandy

The air war against Iraq started a day after the deadline set by the United Nations Security Council for the withdrawal of Iraqi forces from Kuwait (at midnight 15 January 1991). H-Hour for the main attack, or Phase 1, was set for 3.00 am, 17 January (local time); however, the first air operations were initiated, surprisingly not by the US Air Force, but by the US Army. Nine AH-64A Apache helicopters (with one acting as a reserve) were guided to their targets by three air force MH-53J Pave Low helicopters

known collectively as Task Force Normandy. The targets in question were two Iraqi early-warning radar sites based in western Iraq that would have provided highly dangerous advance warnings about coalition air raids into Iraq. Just before H-Hour, 17 January, the Apache helicopters fired Hellfire missiles, Hydra rockets and thousands of 30 mm cannon shells devastating their targets with precise firepower. Unfortunately, although a corridor was opened up in the Iraqi air-defence network for the strike planes over western Iraq, the attack itself was quickly reported back to Baghdad, in effect, providing the advance warning that the strike had been intended to prevent. After completing its mission and receiving the unwelcome attention of Iraqi shoulder-fired missiles (SA-7s) and ground fire, Task Force Normandy returned safely to base.

The F-117A stealth fighter

The bulk of the main attack from 3.00 am onwards could be broken down into three core components that involved stealth aircraft, long-range bombers and conventional fighter-bombers. The F-117A stealth fighter or 'Nighthawk' offered a revolutionary capability to the coalition forces. Its unique design allowed this aircraft to penetrate the most sophisticated of air-defence networks with minimal risk of radar detection. This factor alone meant that these assets could be deployed to targets as single entities without the need for significant aerial support in the form of electronic warfare (EW) planes. Ten stealth fighters from the 415th Tactical Fighter Squadron took off on the night of 17 January from their base at Khamis Mushayt in Saudi Arabia and, armed with 2,000 lb LGBs laser guided bom headed deep into the heart of Iraq. One of their targets, Baghdad itself, was considered so dangerous in terms of its air defences that the F-117A was the only manned aircraft tasked with hitting targets in the Iraqi capital on the initial night of operations. The first strike by the stealth fighters was the Nukhayb air-defence command centre in southern Iraq that was neutralised by these very powerful and deadly accurate bombs. Interestingly, the attack on the telecommunications centre in Baghdad was the most visually stunning strike for coalition planners because CNN was broadcasting its picture through this facility. If the CNN live transmission from Baghdad suddenly went off the air then the strike had been successful. At 3.00 am, in mid-conversation, the CNN reporter's voice from Baghdad was replaced by static.

The longest bombing mission in history

The first night of operations over Iraq witnessed the longest bombing run in history. Seven B-52G bombers were launched in the early hours of 16 January from a base in Louisiana on the mainland of the United States and, 15 hours later, these aircraft dropped 35 AGM-86C ALCMs from their bomb bays before heading home. The accuracy of these missiles with their 1,000 lb warheads was staggering: around 89 per cent hit their targets. Overall, it was a remarkable 14,000-mile (22,500 km) trip that lasted approximately 35 hours. Other B-52G bombers from bases like Diego Garcia in the

Indian Ocean launched conventional bomb attacks on key targets that made the ground shake like a form of man-made earthquake. As in the 'Arc Light' missions in Vietnam (by earlier versions of the B-52), the impact of these strikes on the morale of the average Iraqi soldier on the ground was immense. If the blasts did not kill them, the horrendous concussion waves would.

Air power over Kuwait and Iraq

The largest proportions of the strikes on the first night of operations and thereafter were carried out by conventional fighter-bombers such as F-4G Wild Weasels, to F-111F Aardvarks, F15E Strike Eagles, F-16 C/D Fighting Falcons (the bulk of the attacking aircraft), as well as British and Saudi

The F-111F Aardvarks was one of the most effective but least publicised aircraft during the Gulf War. The F-111 strike aircraft historically had a poor reputation due to developmental problems with earlier models. The F model used against Iraq performed magnificently, particularly because of its advanced night-vision capabilities and targeting system called Pave Tack. It is estimated that the F-111F carried out approximately 3,000 strike missions, with the majority being targeted at Iraqi ground units. (Topham Picturepoint)

The Global Newspaper
Edited and Published
in Paris

Printed simultaneously in Paris,
London, Zürich, Hong Kong,
Singapore, The Hague, Marseille,
New York, Rome, Tokyo, Frankfurt

Herald INTERNATIONAL Tribune

Published With The New York Times and The Washington Post

No. 33,558   **PARIS, FRIDAY, JANUARY 18, 1991**   ESTABLISHED 1887

RELENTLESS ASSAULT

Allied Aircraft Smash Hundreds of Iraqi Targets In Most Intensive Pounding Since World War II

Pilots and flight crew members mingling Thursday on the flight line at a Saudi air base as a radar-jamming U.S. F-4 aircraft returns from a bombing run in Iraq.

1,300 Sorties Flown In 20-Hour Period

As U.S. and allied aircraft backed by waves of cruise missiles continued to smash Iraqi targets Thursday, President George Bush vowed Thursday to keep pounding Iraq ceaselessly until President Saddam Hussein withdrew from Kuwait.

U.S. military officials said more than 1,300 air strikes and 100 cruise missiles hit military targets in the 20-hour period since the bombing started at 3 A.M. local time Thursday.

The Washington Post said the operation, now called Desert Storm, was the most intensive bombardment since World War II.

Chemical Threat Over, French Say, but U.S. Still Sees Risk

Allies' Outlook: Caution and Optimism

By Joseph Fitchett
International Herald Tribune

PARIS — With a well-aimed opening blow, the U.S.-led multinational force seemed on track to knocking out Iraq faster and with less cost than most planners had publicly anticipated.

NEWS ANALYSIS

See TACTIC, Page 4

Scenting Success, World Markets Rally

By Lawrence Malkin
International Herald Tribune

NEW YORK — Stocks and bonds around the world staged huge rallies on Thursday after the threat of an oil shortage was apparently removed by the successful allied air strikes on Iraq.

See MARKETS, Page 12

Debriefing: Day 1

Participants
U.S., British, Saudi, Kuwaiti and French air forces.

Sorties
1,300 sorties were flown by 750 planes in the first 20 hours of the war. Over 100 Tomahawk cruise missiles launched from U.S. warships.

Losses
1 U.S. Navy F-A/18 Hornet strike-fighter. The pilot died.
1 British Tornado GR1 fighter-bomber. Its 2-man crew missing.
1 Kuwaiti jet fighter
1 Iraqi fighter jet. (French military authorities reported that two Iraqi jets had been downed.)

Iraqi Retaliation
Limited initial response, mainly with surface-to-air missiles and anti-aircraft fire. A fire broke out at the Khafji refinery complex in Saudi Arabia when airraiders hit a crude-oil storage tank.

Iraqi Claims
60 allied planes were shot down.
23 Tomahawk cruise missiles recovered, which could be re-used.

Assessment
"So far, so good" — Defense Secretary Dick Cheney. U.S. military intelligence said that 80 percent of the air strikes had been on target.

Other Developments

King Olav of Norway Is Dead at 87

OSLO (Reuters) — King Olav V of Norway, 87, the world's oldest monarch and a symbol of Norwegian resistance to Nazi occupation in World War II, died Thursday of a heart attack, the Royal Palace said. He will be succeeded by his son, Crown Prince Harald, 53, who had assumed the king's official duties since his father suffered a stroke in May.

A senior and terrorists carried out four laser attacks on U.S. installations. *Page 3*

Saddam Hussein on Iraqi television Thursday.

Raids on Atom Plants: Powell Is Satisfied

WASHINGTON — General Colin N. Powell, chairman of the Joint Chiefs of Staff, said Thursday that he was "pleased with the performance" of the allied attacks on chemical and nuclear-weapons facilities inside Iraq.

See ATTACK, Page 4

OPPOSITE Wild Weasel missions (featured on the cover of the *International Herald Tribune*) were highly dangerous and required exceptionally brave pilots. The aim of the mission was to encourage Iraqi radars SAMs to illuminate and/or fire at the aircraft which would then evade the attacks while launching specialised anti-radiation missiles that targeted the SAMs themselves and their all-important command radars. The Americans used HARMs, whereas the British used a highly unusual missile called ALARM which could 'find' the missile sites by itself without having to be directed by the missile pilot. In the event that the Iraqi soldiers turned off their radars, this missile would fly high, deploy a parachute and loiter until a target was acquired. (Edimedia)

BELOW The E-3A AWACS aircraft with its revolving Westinghouse radar played a vital role in the Gulf War. It was the 'eyes in the sky' that could not only co-ordinate around 600 aircraft in the air at any one time but also identify hostile aircraft and vector coalition planes onto them. It was a force multiplier that allowed a greater degree of efficiency to be drawn out of the air campaign and permitted planners on the ground to see the big picture. (TRH Pictures)

Tornadoes. Nearly 700 aircraft attacked Iraq that night with supporting tanker aircraft and, of course, the co-ordinating E-3A AWACS aircraft. The common perception is that the majority of these aircraft carried smart weaponry, but in fact most of the weapons used were plain 'iron' bombs. Less than 10 per cent of the 90,000 tons of ordnance dropped on Iraq were precision-guided munitions (PGM). The lack of Iraqi air opposition had significant ramifications, firstly, for sortie rates, which rose much higher than anticipated, and, secondly, it permitted more time to be devoted to the individual phases of the strategic campaign. Overall, almost 110,000 sorties were flown during the Gulf War and, of these, 44,145 were dedicated to combat. Just 34 Iraqi aircraft were shot down in aerial combat against the coalition forces, around 100 were destroyed on the

ground, others (over 100) fled to Iran, and the rest survived. The Iraqi Air Force barely managed to achieve one aerial combat kill against the armada of aircraft that attacked the country night after night. Even more startling, despite the thousands of SAMs fired, was that radar-guided SAMs shot down only ten coalition aircraft, only 13 were lost to IR SAMs, nine to AAA and one other to enemy fire. The weather proved to be more effective against the air assault than the Iraqi armed forces and, surprisingly, the theatre of operations experienced the worst environmental conditions for 14 years. One historian suggests that poor weather conditions negatively influenced roughly 50 per cent of all sorties against Iraq. Nevertheless, the coalition air strategy devastated the Iraqi armed forces for just over a month before the ground assault began. All phases of the air campaign were accomplished with remarkable precision and, as one observer has commented, the lights in Baghdad did not come on again until after the ceasefire, because the coalition hit the electrical generators on the first night.

The sea war

The coalition naval response was much faster than that of the air and land forces by virtue of the fact that forces were already on hand or near the point of crisis and played a vital yet often forgotten role in the creation of Desert Shield. The tensions in the Gulf in the years prior to Iraq's invasion of Kuwait and the essential requirement to maintain the unimpeded flow of oil to the world had necessitated the creation of naval units

permanently on station in the region. The United States had eight ships of the Joint Task Force Middle East (largely frigates and destroyers) in the waters of the Gulf that could be quickly supported by two-carrier battle groups, the *Independence* (CV 62) in the Indian Ocean and the *Dwight D Eisenhower* (CVN 69) in the Mediterranean Sea. The British also had a small standing force called the Armilla Patrol (usually a frigate or destroyer with supporting assets) in the area as well. The US Navy, as part of

The aircraft-carrier Independence represented the awesome level of technology that the US Navy had achieved by the 1990s. Such ships could carry over 70 combat aircraft and offered more disposable firepower than many air forces in the developing world. They provided the centre-piece of the powerful carrier battle group which included billion-dollar Aegis air-defence cruisers, with their ability to handle mass-missile attacks with counter missiles, and other small escorts like frigates and destroyers. (Topham Picturepoint)

its CENTCOM commitment, had already carefully planned for a contingency such as a threat to the territorial integrity of Saudi Arabia and its response consisted of pre-positioned heavy-lift ships that could support the US Marine Corps as well as the US Army and Air Force for a limited period of time. It had organised the immediate-response support ships into three maritime pre-positioning ship squadrons (MPSSs), two of which were located within striking distance of the Middle East, at

Guam (MPSS3) and even closer at Diego Garcia (MPSS2). A single MPSS could support approximately 16,000 troops in a marine expeditionary brigade (MEB) with all its equipment (tanks, aircraft and ammunition) for at least 30 days of fighting until reinforcements could be brought forward. On 8 August, just six days after the invasion of Kuwait, both MPSSs were dispatched from their bases to support the 7th and 1st MEBs whose troops were flown into the region. After

1st-Lieutenant Baldomero Lopez (T-AK 3010), one of the huge MPSS vessels. (United States Navy)

seven days of sailing, the first ships started off-loading equipment in Saudi Arabia and just ten days later, the entire 7th MEB with 123 tanks and 124 aircraft was ready for operations.

Sea power in the Gulf

The coalition of naval forces included assets provided by Argentina, Australia, Belgium, Canada, Denmark, France, Greece, Italy, Netherlands, Norway, Poland, Portugal, Saudi Arabia, Turkey and Spain. As in the air campaign, the bulk of the forces were contributed by the US Navy which

eventually deployed six-carrier battle groups in support of operations. After the Iraqi invasion of Kuwait, the US Navy appointed Vice-Admiral Henry H. Mauz, Commander 7th Fleet, as the senior naval officer to CENTCOM as COMUSNAVCENT.

ABOVE An F-14 Tomcat, which featured in the film *Top Gun*, takes to the sky to start another combat air patrol over a US carrier battle group. (Topham Picturepoint)

BELOW Row after row of powerful strike aircraft are lined up on the deck of one of America's awesome aircraft carriers. (Topham Picturepoint)

Interestingly, Admiral Mauz, a decorated Vietnam veteran, still retained responsibility for the 7th Fleet and established his headquarters not in Riyadh with CENTCOM but at sea, from two command ships, the *La Salle* (AGF 3) and later the *Blue Ridge* (LCC 19). Surprisingly, despite being on a war footing, the US Navy continued its practice of rotating officers through key posts, as in peacetime. Vice-Admiral Mauz was subsequently replaced by Vice-Admiral Stanley R Arthur on 1 December 1990, just weeks before the air campaign started. Admiral Arthur was an inspired choice on several levels, having been a professional aviator for his entire career and having served with distinction in the air combat over Vietnam.

The integration of the naval air power (predominantly American) with the overall air strategy was not without complications. In Vietnam, the US Air Force and Navy had operated a system called 'route packages' which delineated certain areas of operations to specific forces. To many, particularly the air force, it had been an inefficient use of air power and the navy's suggestion of its use in the Gulf led to a frank exchange of opinions between General Horner and Admiral Mauz (a surface-warfare expert), with the former being completely opposed to it. In addition, the ATO was a much more sophisticated operational tool than anything the US Navy had developed with regard to applying air power against land targets. Having to adopt such a new system in a short period of time meant that the navy lacked the capability to receive the ATO quickly in an electronic format so bulky hard copies had to be distributed to the fleet. Furthermore, ignorance on both sides about the other service was evident, for example, the air force had only a limited understanding of the very powerful Aegis air-defence cruiser with its anti-aircraft-missile capability and the sea-launched Tomahawk missile. These problems were eventually overcome and the arrival of Admiral Arthur certainly helped matters, but relations between the two services had suffered to a degree.

Mine warfare

A critical problem for the US Navy in the Gulf was the relatively small amount of sea space but there was also the threat from Iraqi mines. Mine warfare had been neglected for many years in the US Navy and so its mine-counter-measure (MCM) capabilities rested with one new but untested ship, the *Avenger* (MCM 1), some old 1950s ships, and helicopters, like the MH-53E Sea Dragon, that towed sleds to set off the mines. In comparison, the Royal Navy sent the most advanced MCM ships in the world, the Hunt class, and had a vast amount of experience in these operations. The British naval group under Commodore Christopher Craig occasionally had to vigorously lobby the US Navy to ensure that planning was more sensitive to the requirements of the MCM ships. Nevertheless, during the Gulf War, two US ships, the landing-platform helicopter (LPH) Tripoli (LPH 10) and Aegis cruiser *Princeton* (CG 59) were holed by Iraqi mines on 18 February 1991. In effect, multi-million-dollar ships were seriously damaged by weapons that, in their most basic form, cost just tens of dollars.

Fire from the sea – Tomahawk

The roles of the US Navy in Operation Desert Storm encompassed supporting the air campaign and poising in the Gulf with amphibious forces to persuade Saddam Hussein that a direct assault on Kuwait from the sea was the basis of the coalition ground strategy. On the first night of operations, the US Navy introduced the world to theTomahawk land attack missile TLAM. It represented a combination of new technologies, most notably a turbo-jet engine the size of a basketball, which could power the missile to speeds of around 500 knots, and a terrain-contour-matching system (TERCOM)

The Hunt class MCM ship. One of the most expensive ships, in relative terms, in the Royal Navy. It used a highly innovative glass-reinforced plastic hull that reduced its magnetic signature enormously and carried sophisticated remotely piloted vehicles to neutralise mines. With a mother ship, HMS *Herald* as a logical support vessel, five of these ships made an invaluable contribution to the coalition effort during and after the Gulf War. (Topham Picturepoint)

that allowed Tomahawk to follow a pre-planned route to its target at very low level (often just hundreds of feet above the ground) with unprecedented accuracy. During the war against Iraq, these highly effective missiles had been armed with 1,000 lb conventional warheads and fired from a variety of platforms that included battleships, cruisers, destroyers and nuclear-powered submarines. The great advantage of Tomahawk was that it offered a capability to attack a target deep in enemy territory without the risk of losing a valuable pilot. The first day of Desert Storm witnessed 122 Tomahawks fired, primarily at targets in areas that were considered very dangerous for coalition strike aircraft to attack, particularly Baghdad. Western cameramen in the Iraqi capital were astounded to see these subsonic cigar-shaped missiles calmly flying through the city at very low level, detonating themselves on their targets with deadly precision. Nearly 300 Tomahawks were fired during the Gulf War at a cost of around $1.2 million each.

Strike-carrier warfare

The mighty aircraft-carriers of the US Navy offered a sizeable punch to the combined

The protection of the critical flow of oil in the Gulf was one of the reasons that countries like Britain had provided escorts for the enormous supertankers in the form of the Armilla Patrol since 1980. British warships in concert with their coalition partners played an important part in enforcing the UN embargo on Iraq during Operation Desert Shield. (Topham Picturepoint)

coalition air effort. In terms of strategic deployment, the six-carrier battle groups were divided into two commands: Battle Force Yankee (CTF 155) under Rear-Admiral Riley D. Mixson with the aircraft-carriers *Saratoga* (CV 60) and the *John F Kennedy* (CV 67) in the Red Sea; and the much larger Battle Force Zulu (CTF 154) under Rear-Admiral Daniel P March, stationed in the Gulf and swelling eventually to four aircraft-carriers, *Midway* (CV 41), which relieved *Independence* on 1 November, *Ranger* (CV 61) and later the *Theodore Roosevelt* (CVN 71), which arrived on station on 21 January, and *America* (CV 66), which arrived on station from the Red Sea on 14 February). The array of American carrier air power was impressive: the F-14 Tomcat was one of the most advanced air defence fighters in the world and possessed a radar that could detect targets at 200-nautical-mile distances as well as engaging them at 100-nautical miles out with the Phoenix air-to air missile. Unfortunately, the crowded skies of Iraq (predominantly with coalition planes) and the requirement to have confirmation from at least two different sources (AWACS or other aircraft like the naval E-2C Hawkeye) that planes were hostile meant that the F-14s' remarkable potential for long-range kills was never utilised. Nevertheless, the primary role of these aircraft was to defend the priceless carriers themselves.

First kills to the US Navy

The shorter-range F/A-18 Hornet, used by both the US Navy and Marine Corps, had a greater role in the strikes against Iraqi ground targets and in fact the only aircraft lost in aerial combat over Iraq was flown by Lieutenant-Commander Michael Scott Speicher on the first night of operations. It was suspected that a MiG either shot it down or even collided with it – the details are unclear (even today great mystery still surrounds this incident) because Speicher was assumed killed in the engagement. The first navy air kills of the campaign were by Lieutenant-Commander Mark I Fox and Lieutenant Nick Mongillo of *Saratoga's* VFA-81 air wing on 17 January. Both pilots were flying F/A-18s on a ground-attack mission in western Iraq with two other

aircraft when, just prior to reaching their targets, an E-2C Hawkeye warned them of two hostile MiG-21s flying straight towards them at 15 miles (24 km) out. Both pilots calmly switched their radars from air-to ground mode to air-to-air and Fox, having acquired a target, fired a Sidewinder heatseeker that appeared to lose lock after leaving the aircraft. Milliseconds later, he launched a Sparrow radar-seeking missile but suddenly the Sidewinder reacquired the target and smashed into the MiG-21 with the trailing Sparrow impacting on the remains of the falling aircraft. Concurrently, Mongillo fired a Sparrow missile at the second MiG-21 and destroyed that as well. The engagement time from warning to kill was less than a minute and both pilots successfully resumed their original mission, hitting their targets with 2,000 lb bombs. Surprisingly, these were the only two air combat kills by the US Navy in the entire campaign.

The US Navy deployed several rather old aircraft that had served them well in Vietnam like the A-7 Corsair II, which probably, with the A-10 Warthog, held joint-title for being the least elegantly designed aircraft. One of the

The A-6 Intruder was still a highly valuable aircraft despite its age during the Gulf War. It could launch a variety of specialised ordnance from iron bombs to Rockeyes and missiles. (US Air Force)

most valuable aircraft in the US Navy's inventory was the EA-6B Prowler aircraft which flew electronic warfare (EW) missions or suppressed enemy air defences with either electronic counter-measures (ECMs) or high-speed anti-radiation missiles (HARMs). This aircraft was very effective in these missions and its sister aircraft, the A-6 Intruder was the only naval aircraft that possessed laser designators that allowed it to drop the highly accurate LGBs. Other naval aircraft like the British Tornadoes with the rather old Buccaneers also had to rely on partner aircraft to illuminate the target so that they could drop these bombs. The lack of such equipment reflected a doctrinal difference between the US Navy and Air Force in that the navy preferred low-level strikes whereas, due to the proliferation of AAA and hand-held missiles, the Gulf War demanded a high-level strategy. To emphasise this point, an A-6 Intruder was shot down executing a low-level mining operation over the Zubayr river on 18 January, with the death of both aircrew. Much of the weaponry available to the US Navy, like the Rockeye bomb (a cluster munition), had very significant failure rates in the Gulf War (as much as 40 per cent) because they were dropped from high levels.

The US Marine Corps

At sea, the US Navy sustained thousands of US Marines packed into ships in order to persuade the Iraqi defenders that an amphibious assault was the main attack plan of the coalition forces. The US Marine Corps was led by Lieutenant-General Walter E Boomer as Commanding General, I Marine Expeditionary Force who had earned two silver stars for bravery in Vietnam. The commitment to the Gulf would eventually involve 94,000 Marines of whom approximately 24,000 were kept afloat (4th and 5th MEB and 13th MEU (SOC) under General Harry Jenkins) with the Amphibious Task Force's 31 assault ships. The rest of the marine expeditionary forces (MEFs) (two divisions in strength) was stationed on the border with Kuwait near the coast and was given an integral role in the land battle for Kuwait. In support of the US Marines ashore,

the US Navy brought into the Gulf two very formidable anachronisms, the Iowa class battleships, *Missouri* (BB 63) and *Wisconsin* (BB 64). These ancient mariners had been refurbished in the 1980s with state of the art electronics and weaponry that included Tomahawk cruise missiles and Phalanx close-in weapons. Furthermore, the ships retained their frightening 16-inch guns that could launch a 2,700 lb projectile (about the weight of a small car) 17 miles (27 km) inland and together, the vessels had 18 of these highly powerful guns. The effect of these shells on ground targets was staggering and for the US Marines it was a great comfort having this mobile artillery system lurking off the coastline of Saudi Arabia and Kuwait.

The Bubiyan turkey shoot – destroying the Iraqi Navy

The biggest threat to these vessels was the small but dangerous Iraqi surface fleet and the coastal missile batteries. At sea, as in the air, the resistance of the Iraqi Navy against the coalition forces was very poor. The most famous clash was the so-called 'Bubiyan turkey shoot' that started on 29 January, in which coalition air forces attacked the Iraqi Navy trying to escape, like the Iraqi Air Force, to Iran. For over a day approximately 20 vessels of various types were destroyed by fighter aircraft and helicopters, with only two escaping. The Royal Navy's Lynx helicopters armed with the Sea Skua missile accounted for many of the victims (18 hits from 25 launches) and by 2 February, it was clear that the Iraqi Navy was no longer a significant threat at sea. The last major effort of the Iraqi Navy against the coalition forces occurred on 25 February when a Silkworm missile was launched in the direction of coalition ships, including the *Missouri* but it was destroyed in flight by two Sea Dart missiles fired from the Type 42 destroyer, HMS *Gloucester* (D 96). Again, like the other elements of the Iraqi armed forces, the Navy proved to be a reluctant enemy that gained more success from passive weapons like floating mines rather than offensive operations.

The land war

The land campaign proved to be the shortest part of the Gulf War, yet for planners both in the United States and in Saudi Arabia it was considered the most risky element of Desert Storm. While in the air and at sea the

TOP British troops, bayonets at the ready, on their new SA 80 assault rifles, prepare for action. (Topham Picturepoint)

BOTTOM US troops armed with M-16 assault rifles advance across the desert. The deliberate spacing between the soldiers ensures that in the event of an ambush or the detonation of a mine, only a few people will be injured initially. (Topham Picturepoint)

Light 'pack' artillery in action. These highly versatile guns can be swiftly air transported by helicopters to any position on the battlefield and set up quickly to provide fire support for advancing armour and infantry. (Topham Picturepoint)

coalition had clear numerical and technological superiority, on land, Iraq seemed more of an even match. Given the amount of time that the Iraqi forces had spent preparing their defences in Kuwait, even the most optimistic military commentators expected the coalition forces to incur significant casualties. Yet, the forthcoming land battle in the vast expanses of the Arabian deserts was not the sort of traditional warfare that had been encountered in previous theatres. The harsh experience of Vietnam had encouraged a new generation of military officers to conceptualise warfare in a different way. The new thinking emphasised

manoeuvre warfare, a fluid continuous battlefield, attacks on key enemy weak points and close integration with a dedicated air campaign. These new type of operations came to fruition in the North Atlantic Treaty Organisation (NATO) during the 1980s and became known as the AirLand battle doctrine. When the ground troops were unleashed on Iraqi forces on 24 February 1991, it was the fourth phase (following the three earlier air phases) of operations.

Schwarzkopf and coalition commanders

The coalition forces were fortunate in having an outstanding overall military commander in the form of General H. Norman Schwarzkopf who possessed not only a

personal knowledge of the Middle East (he had lived with his father in Iran after the Second World War) but also the sheer willpower to construct a viable military strategy. The pressures on him were immense: from hawks in Washington, who just wanted him to attack quickly with limited resources, and from the media and international public opinion. In this respect, Desert Shield and Desert Storm benefited enormously from the role played by Lieutenant-General Prince Khalid Bin Sultan al-Saud, Schwarzkopf's Saudi equivalent, who acted as the linchpin between the coalition forces and the Kingdom of Saudi Arabia. The US deputy commander in chief, Lieutenant-General Cal Waller (almost the same size as

General H. Norman Schwarzkopf was one of the finest military officers of his generation to emerge from the élite West Point Military Academy. His size (6 feet 3 inches (1.9 m) and well over 200 lb (90 kg)) made him an imposing figure which, combined with his highly professional approach and keen interest in military history, made a potent combination. Furthermore, he had passed the test of combat extremely well and demonstrated himself to be an exceptionally brave officer, having served two tours in Vietnam with distinction. His nickname, 'Stormin Norman', was derived from his legendary temper that would flare up and die down like a tropical storm. (Topham Picturepoint)

'Stormin Norman'!) bore much of the administrative burden and other allies provided highly capable commanders. The overall British commander in theatre was the highly experienced Lieutenant-General Sir Peter de la Billiere whose distinguished background in the Special Air Service (Special Forces) had provided him with years of operational experience in Arabia. France appointed the equally capable Lieutenant-General Michel Roquejeoffre. Much of the success of the coalition command structure was due to the ability of these key personalities working effectively together despite never having done so before.

The major problem for Schwarzkopf, after receiving the green light for Desert Shield, was having to convert Plan 1002-90 from a defensive strategy (to protect Saudi Arabia with over 200,000 troops) into an offensive operation to liberate Kuwait. Worst-case intelligence estimates suggested that Iraq had over half a million troops in the Kuwaiti theatre of operations which presented CENTCOM with a huge military task (recent research suggests that by the outbreak of the land campaign, this figure, due to desertions and withdrawal of units, in reality may have been halved). Schwarzkopf had to lobby hard with the Bush administration through Colin Powell for the assignment of a second corps, the VII heavy armament (HA) based in Germany, to supplement XVIII Airborne Corps in order to make a proposed attack successful. President Bush authorised the sending of VII Corps on 8 November 1990 and by the start of the ground offensive, CENTCOM had available the equivalent of two US Army corps and one US Marine corps as well as substantial coalition ground forces (over one corps in strength).

Planning for Desert Storm

Strategic thinking on how to liberate Kuwait looked at several options: the first was on direct entry through the 'front door' – a one-corps assault that would thrust straight to the west of Kuwait City beyond the Mutla Pass and seize a defensive position near Al-Jahra. Such an operation would inevitably generate high casualties and leave the relatively small forces vulnerable to counter-attack by the much larger Iraqi forces, despite the offsetting role of the coalition air assets. Another plan that was vigorously lobbied by the US Marine Corps (particularly General Al Gray, Commandant, USMC) right up to the outbreak of the ground offensive was an amphibious assault on the Kuwait coastline. A direct assault on Kuwait City was ruled out relatively quickly due to the fact that it was the obvious point of entry and that the Iraqis had heavily mined the area as well as developing effective defences. Other plans for amphibious landings further down the coast from Kuwait City that would act as forward supply bases gained more acceptance with CENTCOM but events (that is, the short duration of the war) would overtake most of these schemes. The strategy that was finally settled on was a two-corps assault (XVIII and VII Corps) through western Iraq (the 'Hail Mary' left hook) with a thrust along the Kuwaiti coastline by the US Marines (1st MEF) and the Arab coalition forces (Joint Forces Command – North (JFC-N) and Joint Forces Command – East (JFC-E)). This plan would be executed after the air campaign had been initiated and would involve the use of a complex deception plan while over a quarter of a million soldiers shifted, in some cases 300 miles (480 km), westwards to the start-lines for the attack.

The battle of Al Khafji, 29 January 1991

The first major encounter between coalition land forces and the Iraqi Army occurred, quite unexpectedly, before the start of the ground offensive. Why Saddam Hussein decided to attack the Saudi city of Al Khafji near the border with Kuwait on the coastline is still open to speculation but his decision to send one of his better divisions, the 5th Mechanised Division with attached brigades from the 1st Mechanised and 3rd Armoured Divisions caught the coalition by surprise. The strategic significance of seizing Al Khafji was questionable as it possessed no military value (apart from the propaganda coup of

Coalition ground forces

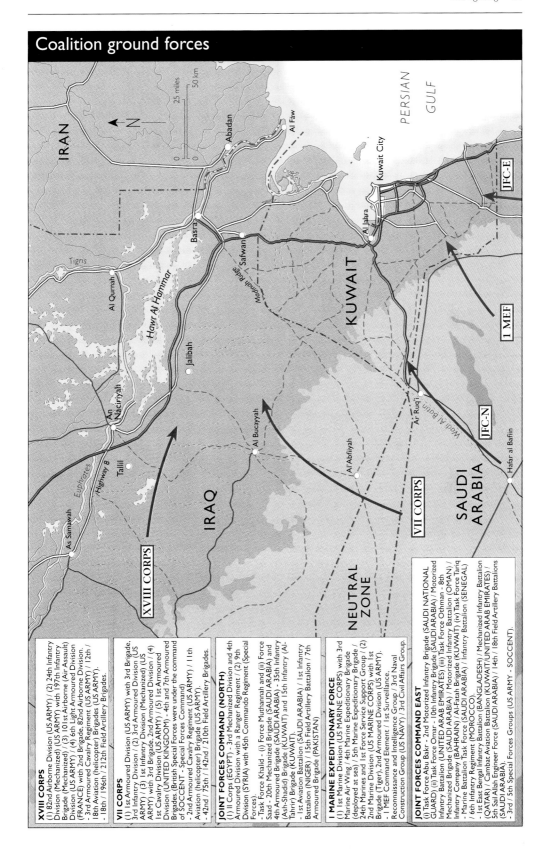

capturing it) and most of the residents had already been evacuated. The initial Iraqi assault went well and the sparse number of coalition troops (US Marines, Special Forces and Saudi forces) were forced to rapidly retreat from the city. From this moment on, the allies quickly regained the initiative. Coalition air power in the form of A-10s, AV-8Bs, AC-130 gunships (with electrically powered gatling guns), F/A-18s, Cobra helicopters and B-52s launched nearly 1,000 sorties, co-ordinated by the remarkable E-8A joint surveillance-and-target-attack radar system (JSTARS), and pounded the three Iraqi columns relentlessly. On the ground, Prince Khalid Bin Sultan al-Saud organised the counter-attack by Saudi and Qatari ground forces that retook the bulk of the city by 31 January. For the Iraqi armed forces, the battle of Al Khafji was nothing short of a disaster. Only 20 per cent of the division (that had possessed around four hundred

E-8A JSTARS was still in the development stage when two of the planes (variant of the Boeing 707) were sent to the Gulf. These planes carried a synthetic-aperture radar that provided almost real-time battlefield intelligence on the enemy movements on the ground over an area about the size of the Kuwaiti theatre of operations. JSTARS suffered many teething problems during the Gulf War but when they worked, as they did during the battle of Al Khafji and the Iraqi retreat from Kuwait, it provided coalition commanders with a view of the battlefield that had previously not been possible. (Topham Picturepoint)

strikes, just over half were aimed at Saudi Arabia, about three at Bahrain and the rest at Israel. The first launches hit Israel on 17 January and from then on caused immense social panic to the extent that four people died of heart attacks. In fact, despite receiving around 40 missiles, only two people died directly as a result of the strikes, with just over 200 wounded. Militarily speaking, these launches were completely ineffective but politically they had the potential to be immensely damaging because they brought Israel to the point of entering the conflict, which would have split the coalition. The US solution to this problem was to rush Patriot anti-ballistic missiles to Israel. The performance of this missile still generates a great deal of speculation as to whether it was an effective system or not. At the time, the US Army claimed that Patriot hit 45 out of the 47 Scuds at which it was launched, at but some post-war analysis suggested it had hit no warheads at all. Its effectiveness may be in question but, psychologically, it was very reassuring to troops in Saudi Arabia and citizens in Israel to watch Patriot missiles responding to the incoming Scuds.

In addition to the Patriot system, the coalition forces turned to two types of assets to reduce Iraq's ability to fire these missiles in what was called the 'Scud hunt'. The first type used aircraft like F-15s as well as A-10s to track down and destroy the Scud's mobile transporter, erector and launchers (TELs) day and night. The Scud B had a limited range of just 175 miles (280 km) but modified versions like the Al-Hussein could reach 370

tanks and armoured personnel carriers) made it back across the border to the Iraqi Third Corps from where the attack had originated.

Scud missiles and Special Forces

Iraq's use of its surface-to-surface ballistic missiles caused enormous political and military consternation at the time but in the cold light of the coalition victory it actually achieved very little. Saddam's regime managed to fire just 91 missiles. Of these

miles (600 km) so planners divided the areas most likely to contain TELs into two 'Scud boxes'. Question marks again hang over the success rate of coalition air power against mobile Scud launchers because it was like searching for a needle in a haystack, and from the air the poor weather compounded the difficulty of finding the missiles. The second type of assets were Special Forces (British and American). These highly specialised unconventional warriors aroused great scepticism as to what they could bring to the Gulf region that other conventional units could not. The Scud dimension offered a scenario at a time when the land forces were not ready to fight, but Special Forces

The Patriot missile had a range of 37 miles (60 km) and could engage targets between 400 feet (122 m) and 13.5 miles (22 km). Scuds were often detected at ranges of over 100 miles (160 km) away and intercepted when the distance closed to 6–18 miles (10–29 km). Each missile cost just under $700,000 each. (US Air Force)

Map key
1   The bulk of Iraq's forces were located either in or around Kuwait, clearly revealing that Saddam anticipated either an amphibious assault or a thrust up the coastline.
2   Neutral Zone. (The spacing of the Iraqi forces is not to scale).
3   The Republican Guard divisions are all named and represented Saddam's most powerful forces.

Iraq's ground forces on the eve of the coalition offensive

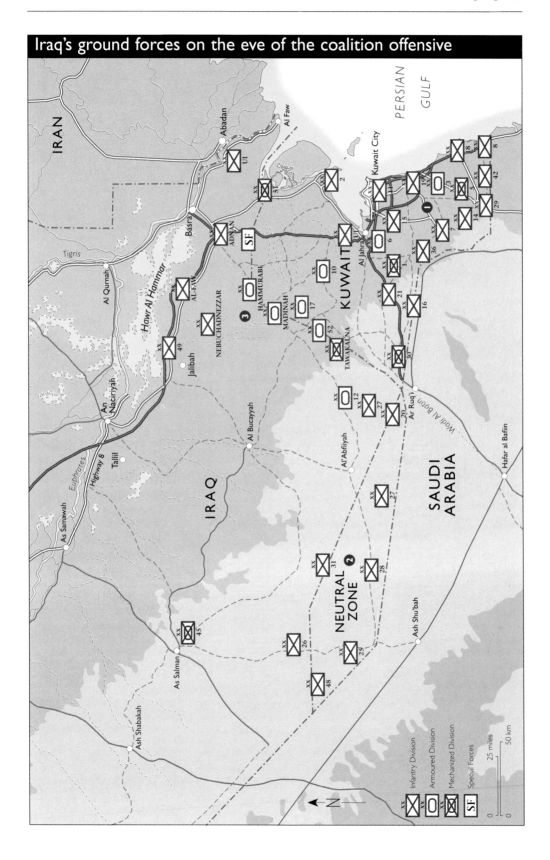

A Scud missile and launcher. (Edimedia)

The most deadly Scud attack in Saudi Arabia occurred when a missile hit a US barracks on 25 February killing 28 and wounding just under 100 US service personnel.

were available for missions deep inside Iraqi territory. Initial liaison with air assets was difficult while trying to vector the aircraft on to the Scud TELs before they moved or fired, but this improved over time. The domination of the main supply routes by Special Forces within the Scud boxes is claimed by General De La Billiere to have forced the Scuds beyond the effective launch range of the missile (that is, deeper into Iraq) after 26 January and so halted firings against Israel.

The ground offensive

The ground offensive began at 4.00 am local time on 24 February 1991. XVIII Airborne Corps under the command of Lieutenant-General Gary Luck led the attack. His formation was positioned on the western flank of VII Corps and was tasked to advance just under 185 miles (300 km) into Iraq to the Euphrates river in order to block major crossing points and prevent the reinforcements heading into Kuwait from Iraq. In addition, elements from his command of well over 100,000 troops would interdict Iraqi troops heading along the major road called Highway 8 and assist in the destruction of the Republican Guard. On the first day of operations, the French 6th Light Armoured Division seized the strategic objective; Rochambeau and the 101st US Airborne Division pushed forward in a classic helicopter assault and took Objective Cobra (93 miles (150 km) away). This strategic position was turned into a forward operating base (fuel and other supplies) while additional soldiers from the 101st flew on to cut off Highway 8. Concurrently, as these swift-air-assault units seized their objectives, mechanised forces (101st) headed towards Cobra to consolidate the position. By the

end of the first day, XVIII Corps had managed remarkable progress, having established forces 170 miles (273 km) into Iraq and a notable characteristic of the day's operations was the thousands of Iraqi troops who quickly surrendered after short engagements with the coalition forces. The highly successful advance of the airborne elements of XVIII Corps persuaded Schwarzkopf to speed up the overall operation, given the willingness of the Iraqi forces to surrender. The heavy element of XVIII Corps, the 25,000-strong 24th Infantry Division (Mechanised), led by the aggressive Major-General Barry McCaffrey, was ordered to attack its objectives (Brown, Red and Gray) five hours earlier than had been planned and advanced 75 miles (120 km) on the first day with minimal opposition. By 25th February, this division had moved 84 miles (135 km) into Iraq, having smashed the Iraqi 26th and 35th Infantry Division, and now prepared to shift eastwards to take on the Republican Guard.

Exploiting the breakthrough

The attack by VII Corps (the heavy armor) under the command of Lieutenant-General Fred Franks was accelerated by 15 hours to the afternoon of the first day of the offensive (24 February) rather than the early hours of day two (25 February). VII Corps had almost 150,000 soldiers at its disposal and each division had nearly 400 heavy tanks along with thousands of other vehicles of every description. The mission of VII Corps was to destroy the Republican Guard and trap the Iraqi forces in Kuwait. The battle plan for this corps was quite challenging, involving the 1st Cavalry Division (the reserve division) attacking the eastern-most flank of VII Corps' area of responsibility to persuade the concentrated Iraqi forces that this was the main assault when, in fact, that was taking place on the western flanks and in the centre. Meanwhile, the 2nd Armoured Cavalry Regiment and the 1st and 3rd Armoured Divisions would cross the Iraqi lines on the western flank, heading towards objective

The ground offensive (24 February 1991)

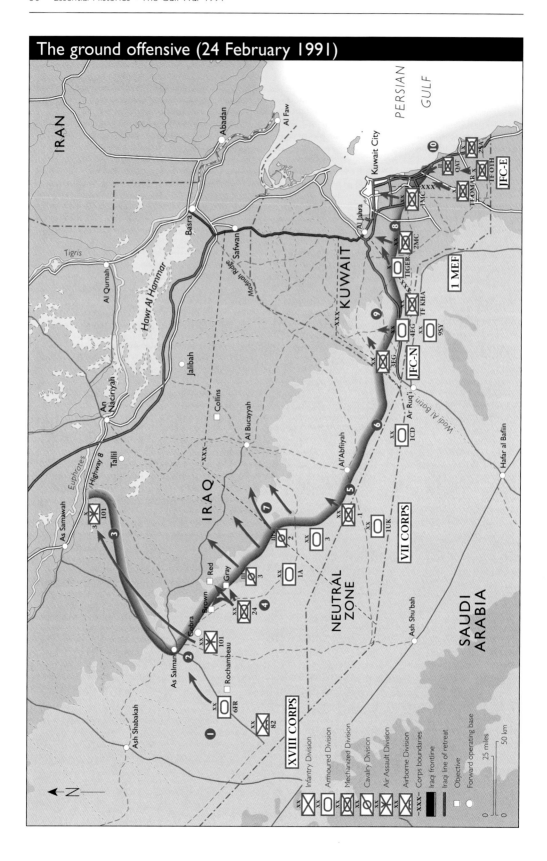

'Collins' and the 1st US Infantry Division (the 'Big Red One') would breach the centre position through which would pass the British 1st Armoured Division.

The major attacks were preceded by a short artillery barrage of about 30 minutes in which over 10,000 shells and more than half a million 'bomblets' (from rockets) rained on the Iraqi positions. In the west, the attacking forces quickly overwhelmed the Iraqi defenders and made rapid progress northwards. Towards the centre, the 1st US

Infantry Division using M1A1 tanks fitted with mine ploughs smashed through the defensive line (in many cases burying Iraqi soldiers alive) and opened up wide breaches. It quickly defeated two Iraqi divisions (the 48th and 26th) by applying superior firepower and tactics as well as accumulating significant numbers of prisoners. Moving an entire armoured corps through these breaches was by no means easy and despite the initial quick success, General Franks was forced to temper the desire of CENTCOM for a swift advance with the requirement of his corps to move forward as a concentrated body rather than in separate elements. Therefore, on the first night, he stopped his advance units from going any further until his main forces were through the breach.

Joint Force Command North (JFC-N) was sandwiched between VII Corps and the 1st MEF. The mission of the combined Egyptian, Saudi and Kuwaiti forces (with the Syrians in reserve) was to push over the Iraqi defences, protect the right flank of VII Corps and seize key positions inside of Kuwait. Being a new command, this formation moved cautiously forward in the afternoon of G-Day and attacked objectives at a slow pace. In contrast, the marines of the 1st MEF under the command of Lieutenant-General Boomer embraced their very difficult task with typical enthusiasm and momentum. CENTCOM required the marines to overcome the Iraqi forces in Kuwait and advance on the Mutla Pass in order to convince Saddam Hussein that this was the main assault. 1st MEF divided the attack between its two divisions, with the 1st Marine Division attacking towards the Al-Jabir airfield with the 2nd Marine Division (with the US Army's Tiger Brigade having replaced the British 1st Armoured Division reallocated to VII Corps) to its

FOLLOWING SPREAD The MLRS has a maximum range of 20 miles (32 km). Each M-77 rocket contains 644 bomblets and 12 rockets can be fired in less than 60 seconds to cover a specified area with just under 7,728 bomblets. Approximately 10,000 MLRS rockets were fired during the Gulf War. (TRH Pictures)

west, pushing upwards towards Mutla Pass.
(Joint Force Command East (JFC-E) was
given a coastal path towards Kuwait and its
assortment of Arab units, US Special Forces
and marine advisers helped to co-ordinate
air strikes and battleship gunfire support
for their advance. The progress of this force
was highly impressive and had achieved all
of its objectives on the first day. All three
elements, JFC-N, 1st MEF and JFC-E had
considerably less armour than VII Corps
but made up for it with light vehicles,
anti-tank missiles and excellent close
air support.

The push forward

By the second day of operations, XVIII
Airborne Corps was making steady progress
in the west and had now reached its
blocking positions, and the 24th Infantry
Division (Mechanised) was ready to swing
eastwards to close the door on the Iraqi
forces. VII Corps was making less progress
by being still short of Objective 'Collins'.
Schwarzkopf, seeing the bigger picture and
aware that the Iraqi forces were on the
verge of folding, was enormously frustrated
by the inability of VII Corps to move
swiftly, so he placed great pressure on the
commander-in-chief of all US Army forces
in the Gulf, Lieutenant-General John
Yeosock to push Franks forward. At
'Collins', VII Corps would wheel eastwards
to form the left hook and crash into the
major Republican Guard units. By the end
of the day, many of the key units, 1st US
Armoured Division, 2nd Armoured Cavalry
Regiment and the 3rd Armoured Division
were ready to attack the Republican the
following day. For the British 1st Armoured
Division under the command of Major-
General Rupert Smith, 25 February saw the
start of its offensive on objectives named
after metals, for example, 'Brass', with each
brigade (7th and 4th) attacking respective
targets in sequence. The British line of
assault represented another giant left hook
that would take them from Iraq to the
Kuwaiti coastline. Much of the fighting
(like the American experience) was swift

and the Iraqi forces were soon enveloped,
but tragedy struck on 26 February when
coalition A-10 aircraft mistakenly attacked
two British Warrior vehicles, killing nine
soldiers and wounding 11. On their flanks,
JFC-N continued advancing at a slow but
steady pace whereas the marines had to
move forward under the twin pressures of
poor visibility (the Iraqi forces had set fire
to the oil wells in Kuwait) and significant
opposition from the enemy. Both the 1st
and 2nd Marine Divisions experienced
co-ordinated Iraqi counter-attacks in which
tanks often engaged each other at short
range due to the masking effects of
immense amounts of smoke. But, by the
end of the day, the marines were just 10
miles (16 km) away from Kuwait City. JFC-E
had a much easier advance than the
marines with very little opposition. Like
XVIII Corps and VII Corps, these units had
a logistical problem dealing with the large
numbers of Iraqis who were more than
willing to surrender.

Attacking the Republican Guard

On 26 February the coalition battle plan
come to fruition as the XVIII and VII
Corps lined up in a rough curve from the
Euphrates to the Saudi border to head
eastwards in a charge forward into the

Map key
1   The French 6th Light Division captures As Salman
    and elements of the 82nd Airborne Division help
    defeat the 45th Infantry Division. The 82nd starts
    moving forward to Cobra.
2   The 24th Infantry Division (Mechanised) and the 3rd
    Armoured Cavalry Regiment push forward into Iraq
    destroying opposing elements from the 24th and
    35th Infantry Divisions.
3   The heavy units of VII Corps now start to swing left
    towards Objective 'Collins' in order to smash into the
    Republican Guard units.
4   JFC-N starts to make better progress, especially Task
    Force Khalid.
5   The I MEF has to fight the environment (black acrid
    smoke from the burning Kuwaiti oil fields) and the
    retreating Iraqi forces that still counterattack in
    numbers. After more intense fighting, I MEF is just
    10 miles from Kuwait City.
6   JFC-East faces less opposition than I MEF and
    continues to make good progress.

The left hook (25 February 1991)

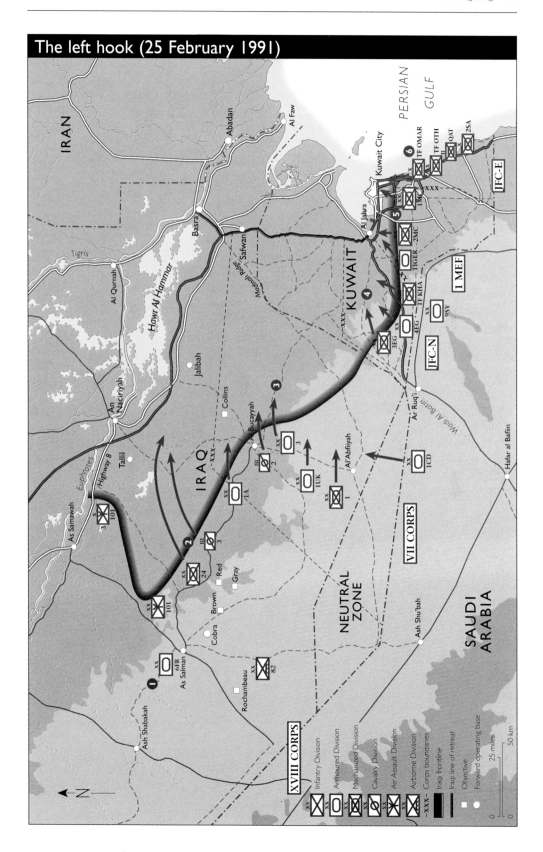

Republican Guard. To the north on Highway 8, the 101st was still hitting Iraqi convoys along the road. Immediately south of them, the 82nd Airborne Division guarded the lines of communication for the allied forces. To the north-east of the 82nd, the 24th Infantry Division Mechanised and the 3rd Armoured Cavalry Regiment manoeuvred eastwards, trying to close off the Euphrates escape route. The fighting became more intense as these units encountered Iraqi commando forces that were willing to engage in close combat. VII Corps now closed on the main Republican Guard divisions (Hammurabi, Madinah and Tawakalna). The 1st US Armoured Division (with the later assistance of the 3rd Armoured Division) attacked the Tawakalna Division throughout the afternoon and evening of 26 February. The attacks were more difficult than previous assaults because the Republican Guard had chosen good defensive positions and the weather was extremely poor as well, with high winds playing havoc with sighting equipment. These conditions forced the 3rd Armoured Division to close with the enemy and it had neutralised the Tawakalna Division by the early hours of the next day. To the south, the 2nd Armoured Cavalry Regiment encountered a larger enemy force of tanks and fought a battle over four hours, in which time, the superior firepower of the Americans (tanks, artillery and Apache helicopters) devastated the Iraqis. Further south, the British 1st Armoured Division engaged the Iraqi 52nd Armoured Division in a sandstorm (another four-hour battle) until destroying the position. To the right of these forces, JFC-N had increased its pace considerably by 26 February and headed towards Kuwait City with minimal opposition. The 1st MEF had fought some tough engagements with the Iraqi forces and now turned their attention to the final objectives. The 1st Marine Division had attacked Kuwait International Airport the previous night and, having won the battle, moved to take

it by early morning. The 2nd Marine Division with the Tiger Brigade pushed towards Mutla Ridge and in the process fought stiff battles with units from the Iraqi 3rd Armoured and 5th Mechanised Divisions. Air power allowed the marines and the Tiger Brigade to take the Mutla Ridge by the end of the day and further to the east, JFC-E maintained its rapid advance to Kuwait City, which it reached comfortably.

The battle of Madinah Ridge

XVIII Airborne Corps now released 24th Infantry Division (Mechanised), having placed the 3rd Armoured Cavalry Regiment under the control of General McCaffrey, to attack Al Jalibah and Tallil airfields and proceed eastwards towards Basra. Having detailed units to attack the airfields, this combined force either shot its way through or went around scattered units from various Republican Guard divisions (Al-Faw, Hammurabi and Nebuchadnezzar) at an average speed of 40 mph (65 kmph) until it met up with VII Corps along Highway 8. Behind this ambitious rapid advance the 101st Airborne Division seized another forward-operating base called 'Viper' several hundred miles to the east of Cobra to help support future operations. VII Corps finally closed on the remaining Republican Guard divisions in its sector (Adnan, Al Madinah, Hammurabi and the remnants of the Tawakalna). The 1st US Armoured Division engaged a variety of different Iraqi units, predominantly the Madinah Division, in an area that became known as 'Madinah Ridge' because this Republican Guard formation had laid a trap for the Americans by placing their tanks in concealed positions on high ground. Unfortunately for the Republican Guard, the 1st Armoured Division detected their presence and engaged them at distances that far out-ranged the Iraqi T-72 tanks with tank fire, artillery and air power. The failed trap turned into a bloodbath with 300 Iraqi armoured vehicles being destroyed for the loss of just two Americans (including one killed by his own side by accident). The 1st Infantry Division, at the same time, had fought its way through to the Kuwait City–Basra Highway before heading north towards a position just south of Safwan, and the British 1st Armoured Division was ordered into Kuwait over the Wadi Al-Batin, towards their final objective. JFC-N had by this

stage reached the outskirts of Kuwait City and that morning the Kuwaiti contingent led them into the capital. The 1st MEF consolidated the positions of the 1st and 2nd Marine Divisions which remained the same until the ceasefire the next day. JFC-E was ordered into the city at the same time. By the evening of 27 February, the battle for Kuwait was effectively over.

Map key (page 67)

1 French forces still provide security for the coalition forces in Western Iraq.
2 A new forward operating base called Viper is seized by the 2nd Brigade of the 101st Air Assault Division just south of Jalibah airfield.
3 The 24th Infantry Division and the (now attached) 3rd Armoured Cavalry Regiment push aggressively eastwards. Their position so close to the retreating Iraqi forces outside of Basra by the ceasefire (the following day) would lead to the clash between the 1st Brigade, 24th Infantry (Mechanised) and the Hammurabi Division on 2 March.
4 Safwan airfield became the chosen site for the negotiations between the coalition and Iraqi forces.
5 The immense destruction of Iraqi vehicles on the road to Basra caused the media to label it 'the highway of death'.
6 The first forces officially into Kuwait City were the Kuwaitis forces in JFC-N. The advancing forces of 1 MEF held back and let the Arab pass into the city while they consolidated their positions. The Arab forces of JFC-E also moved into the city.

Map key (Page 66)

1 The 82nd Airborne Division moves to a covering position east of Cobra.
2 The 24th Infantry Division (Mechanized) sends its 197th Brigade to attack Tallil airfield while the 1st Brigade heads east along Highway 8 towards Basra with the 2nd Brigade heading towards Jalibah airfield. The 3rd Armoured Cavalry Regiment also heads eastwards. All of these units encounter stiff resistance.
3 The US 1st Armoured Division attacks the Tawakalna Division in the late afternoon/ evening.
4 The 3rd Armoured Division joins the fight and the battle rages throughout the evening and early hours of 27 February but the superior equipment, training and weaponry (artillery, tanks, A-10 aircraft and Apache helicopters) proves decisive. The 2nd Armoured Calvary Regiment also engages elements of the Tawakalna Division.
5 The British 1st Armoured Division defeats the 52nd Armoured Division after a battle lasting four hours and heads towards Objective Tungsten on the Kuwaiti border.
6 The collapse and retreat of the Iraqi forces allows the 1st Cavalry Division to be retasked to join the attack against the Republican Guard that requires it to move just under 300 km to the north-east in 24 hours.
7 JFC-N makes much better progress towards Kuwait City as the Iraqi forces start retreating en masse for the Iraqi border.
8 The 2nd Marine Division and the Tiger Brigade head towards Mutla Ridge and inflicts heavy damage (with air support) on the retreating Iraqi forces.
9 The 1st Marine Division also generates immense attrition on Iraqi units before seizing the international airport.
10 JFC-E manages to reach Kuwait City itself.

Attacking the Republican guard (26 February 1991)

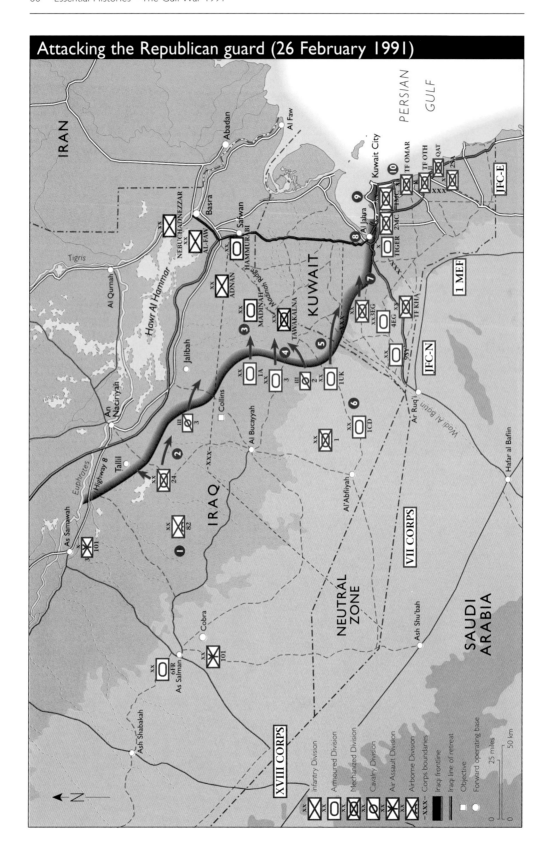

Victory (27 February 1991)

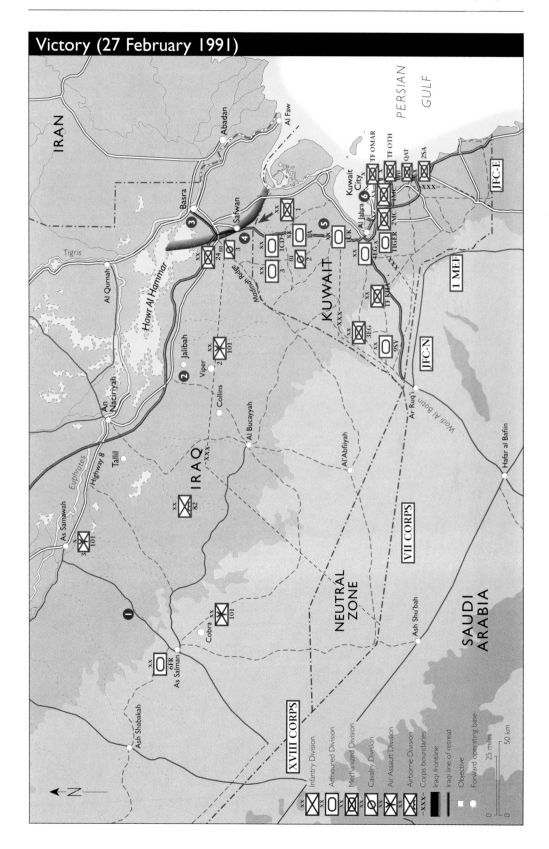

Lieutenant Alex Vernon, 24th Infantry Division (Mechanised)

Desert Shield

Lieutenant Alex Vernon was a typical example of a young officer who found himself (almost overnight) in the hot deserts of Saudi Arabia. His unit, the 24th Infantry Division (Mechanised), was a core formation of CENTCOM whose role was to swiftly deploy to the Middle East in the event of a crisis. Like many competent but inexperienced junior officers (he had not yet faced the test of combat), Alex discovered, on hearing that he was going to deploy to Saudi Arabia, that many of his personal fears bubbled to the surface. The routine preparations for deployment brought with them the sense of the inevitable, as soldiers stood in line for inoculations and medical examinations, in other words being 'processed' for war – a deeply depersonalising experience in which the individual becomes merely a military asset, to be cleaned, polished and used like a rifle. For a young lieutenant just a few years out of the élite West Point Military Academy, the prospect of going to war was an immensely challenging notion: would he perform well? would men under his command die because of him? All these thoughts loomed large in his mind prior to deployment. The 24th Infantry Division (Mechanised) prepared and loaded their tanks (literally stuffing the turrets with bags full of kit) and putting them on ships lying in the Savannah river for the long trip to the Middle East. The troops themselves would then fly on to Saudi Arabia and await the arrival of their equipment. Just before boarding the plane, each soldier was offered a small bible (Alex took one), a plastic bag containing water, sun cream with other small toiletries and a miniature American flag.

The heat in Saudi Arabia, 105ºF (40ºC) in the late afternoon, was the first thing that hit the soldiers when walking off the plane at Dammam Airport. Their home for the next few days would be a tent city in the port itself while they waited for the fast merchant ships to arrive with their equipment. On 28 August, just over two weeks after sailing from the United States, the first ships arrived and the 24th Infantry Division (Mechanised) eventually deployed to a place called Assembly Area Hinesville, south of An Nu'ayriyah on huge heavy-equipment transport systems (vehicles that carried tanks) 225 miles (140 km) west of Dammam. Conditions were very difficult in the desert. Everyone was constantly sweating, the sand was too hot to touch and sleeping was often uncomfortable in the heat. The enemy was not so much the Iraqis but dehydration. It made the smallest task an effort, suppressed the desire to eat, made soldiers weaker and had the potential to kill if not constantly fended off by drinking huge amounts of bottled water. Then sandstorms (which often lasted for hours) would force the soldiers to take refuge as well as bake in their tanks (Abrams M-1) and afterwards have to clean the external weapons that were clogged with sand. The notion of having a quiet night's sleep outside of the tanks was also dispelled by the threat of snakes and insects which would get too close for comfort. From these very primitive conditions, tents, latrines and rudimentary showers would be slowly added to make life more bearable and, as the season changed to winter, one of the major problems would be the freezing nights as well as the odd rain shower. Food poisoning from local food was another environmental hazard and at one stage 40 per cent of the troops in Saudi Arabia suffered from severe bouts of diarrhoea caused local bacteria and fortunately treatable with ciprofloxicin.

In his memoirs, Alex Vernon spends a great deal of time talking about the various methods of staying in touch with his girlfriend Maria and the family back in the United States. Telephones were initially rare, just a single phone by a gas station, until AT&T set up a 48-unit telephone bank in the nearby town of As Sarrar. He recalls one conversation:

From the gas station the morning of 30 October I woke her, catching her completely by surprise: 'Al? ... Al? ... I love you ... I love you' – her first words to me. I still feel them, I wrote to her the next day. I still feel them as I write this sentence today. Outside the store an Arab civilian sat against the corner of the building with an automatic rifle, magazine inserted, and a magazine belt slung over his shoulder. Some American GIs drove by in a Mazda 626.

AT&T also provided a fax service that was used so much by Maria that she was dubbed 'the Desert Faxtress'. Soldiers tried all sorts of methods to make communication with 'back home' more real and some experimented with voice recordings. But for many, it was just too painful to listen with their loved ones this way. Such was the fascination with receiving the mail that Alex Vernon wrote his only poem about it:

A Desert Shield soldier, to his mistress
Arabia offers a paucity of pulchritudinous pleasures:
No bikinied bunnies on beaches,
No glossy 2-D festal virgins.

I receive a Playboy in a Pringles can:
Americans cannot live without America,
So my friends send this piece of her.

Peace – her peace, her salaciously splayed solitude:
Packages pour from her;
She delivers.

Only she slakes me:
My odalisque, my Madonna;
America, the beautiful.

Desert Storm

Alex Vernon's fears grew, naturally, as the likelihood of the ground offensive of Operation Desert Storm became more and more real. In an extract from a letter to Maria on 10 January 1991, he reveals the effect of the mounting pressure:

We are, it seems, bound for war. Greg says he is 'resolute.' Bob at least can smile. Matt has not changed. I am terrified.

I had three letters from Mom, all from Christmas time. I read them, in my tent, and started crying. I left the tent and ran into Lt Novak, who had come to visit. I chased her off, 'too busy packing'.

I am terrified. We are packing our gear. Most stuff the army will take from us in the next few days; it leaves us with our 'go to war' gear. All the latrines in the company but one, and all the showers and heaters but one, disappeared today. Tomorrow we begin wearing our chemical suits, flak vests, and steel pots as our regular uniform.

I cannot handle this. I am not cut out for it. All I want to do is cry. Nothing makes sense. I think I wrote earlier that knowing the plan set me somewhat at ease, because I knew something. Well I was wrong. Now I see that I know nothing of the future. Nothing. It is the most terrifying vision, this black hole of a future. It's sucking me close, and I cannot see through it, or behind it. I see pure blackness; that is my future.

Clearly, the strain of uncertainty about the future had come to the fore and few soldiers in history can boast that they did not have such doubts on the eve of battle nor felt the helplessness of the individual in the face of powerful impersonal forces like armies. Despite his understandable worries, Alex Vernon carried out his duty as an officer in the US Army and, on 24 February 1991, he rolled across the Iraqi border as part of 24th Infantry Division

(Mechanised). In contrast to earlier letters, his account of a incident in the battle for Jalibah airfield on 27 February reveals how professionalism replaced sensitivity while fighting:

I didn't see the sandbag-covered bunker directly in the tank's path until we were too close to fire it up with a HEAT round, and the coax machine gun would have been ineffective against such a deep and fortified position. I could try and dodge it, potentially screwing the formation behind us and allowing Iraqi infantry to pop out of the bunker after we passed, with easy shots at our rear; I could attempt to straddle the bunker, exposing the tank's thin underbelly to whoever inhabited the bunker; or I could order my driver to aim one tread at the bunker and squash it. 'Hit the bunker, Reynolds. Crush it.' We hardly noticed the bump.

Alex Vernon passed the test of combat and during this battle was fired upon, hearing bullets bouncing off the hull of his tank. His 70-ton Abrams M1A1 tank was a powerful vehicle of war that fired 120 mm armour-piercing rounds (made from depleted uranium) that were called 'magic bullets' because they had such a devastating effect on enemy tanks. The 24th Infantry Division (Mechanised) saw a great deal of action in the Gulf War, led by their dynamic commander, Major-General Barry McCaffrey, and found itself not far from Basra by the ceasefire. A few weeks later, Alex Vernon was on a plane back to America and the life that he had missed so much in the deserts of Arabia. A surprising feature of modern-day life is that through the marvels of the jet age, soldiers can be whisked within a matter of hours from an intense theatre of war (in which the threat to life is very high) to an ecstatic national homecoming. The switch from one environment to the other so quickly is often a disorientating experience – socially and emotionally. For his service, he was awarded the 'Army Commendation Medal with V-Device' (valour in combat) and left the army just a few months later. His own commentary about the effect of the war is revealing yet familiar to many veterans:

I returned from the war selfish. The world had robbed me, and now it owed me. I bought the convertible, gave Maria up, chased skirts, then spent the three months after my resignation unemployed, making and breaking and making and breaking an engagement to another woman. The next three years, finally in graduate school at the University of North Carolina at Chapel Hill, were very much a recovery from the war and postwar period of my life.

Dr Alex Vernon is now an Assistant Professor of English at Hendrix College in Arkansas and has written his memoirs along with five other colleagues (see 'Further reading').

The Eyes of Orion (Kent, Ohio 1999) with permission of the Kent State University Press.

Lieutenant Alex Vernon of 24th Infantry Division (Mechanised). (With permission of Alex Vernon)

The global impact of the Gulf War

The Gulf War was an unusual campaign in comparison with previous military actions in recent history because it directly and indirectly involved a multitude of nations from several continents; also it was relatively short once the shooting started and was located in one of the most remote locations in the world. Internationally, despite the blanket coverage by CNN, the geographical remoteness of the campaign created in some ways a sense of detachment in those viewing the events from afar, a separateness from the everyday aspects of world affairs. Some writers have even questioned whether the Gulf War occurred at all and have suggested that it was an enormous act of simulation or 'virtual' warfare. This argument is premised on the idea that images of the fighting in the deserts of Iraq and Kuwait were noticeably different from images of warfare seen previously. Pictures of dead bodies, mangled flesh and widespread civilian destruction had been replaced by video footage of clinically precise strikes on equipment (not personnel) and purely military facilities. The Gulf War appeared to offer a new, cleaner type of war that raised questions in the minds of critics as to whether it could be accurately described as warfare or was just an elaborate form of military simulation.

In the United States, the reality of the war to the Bush administration was not in doubt, since the US had created the massive coalition of forces in Saudi Arabia and supplied the bulk of the forces. For America, the political and economic stakes were high. The world's largest and most powerful economy needed to keep oil supplies flowing from the Middle East to maintain the high levels of consumerism that its average citizen took for granted. At the same time, deploying military forces was a huge risk given the uneven performance of US troops in Vietnam and the fear of the predicted 7,000 deaths and 20,000 wounded. Another disaster on the scale of that in south-east Asia in the 1970s would have had dire consequences. Confidence in the United States would have plunged (with a consequential impact on the stock markets) and its standing in world affairs would also have seriously declined. The United States had a great deal to prove in the deserts of Arabia, not only militarily but also in the light of the post-Cold-War environment, to maintain its position internationally as the only remaining superpower in the world. For post-modernists the Gulf War may have been a 'virtual' war but for the families of the half a million troops in the Middle East, the nature of the conflict was very different. When nations go to war, old traditions re-emerge within society. Wives of soldiers again tied yellow ribbons around trees and letter writing was taken up with new-found enthusiasm (bearing in mind the poor communications with Saudi Arabia initially). The United States that sent off and welcomed back the troops from the fighting in the Gulf was very different to the country that condemned its soldiers to fight in Vietnam and castigated them even more when they came back – and this just a generation before. Financially, the war against Iraq must represent one of the most cost-effective campaigns in US history because the bulk of the war stocks already existed from the Cold War and its allies, particularly Kuwait and Saudi Arabia, contributed the majority of the funds for the military costs. The Gulf War gave back America some of the pride that it had lost in the jungles of Vietnam but, more importantly, to a nation obsessed with winning (whether it be in business, politics or sport) it gave a decisive military victory which the people had not savoured since the Second World War.

In Europe, reactions were quite mixed towards events unfolding in the Middle East. Britain, as the strongest ally of the United States, staunchly joined the military campaign under the direction of its Prime Minister, Margaret Thatcher (who ironically became the best-known British casualty, not to Iraqi bullets but rather to those of her own Conservative Party) and ended it with John Major in power. The British Parliament did contain some loud dissenters over Britain's involvement in the Gulf War but the vast majority supported the official Government line. For the British armed forces, Operation Granby was the biggest operational deployment since the Second World War with just under 45,000 personnel. Overall, relations with CENTCOM were good, apart from an incident in London on 2 January 1991 when a Royal Air Force officer left a computer containing an outline of the war plan in his car. The computer was subsequently stolen. Despite this setback, the British and Americans continued to work well together. Surprisingly, the most noticeable effect of the Gulf War on British society was the number of books by former members of the Special Forces (usually about 'failed' missions) that dominated the literature in the years after the conflict. In France, the commitment to the US-led coalition was characterised at times by contradictory signals. France had been a very close supporter of Iraq and many French politicians had interests in the Iraqi regime, and this created significant internal pressure to remain on the sidelines. Nevertheless, President François Mitterrand moved slowly towards the US position, initially committing an aircraft-carrier, the aged *Clemenceau*, and then a light armoured division to an operation known as 'Daguet'. His defence minister, Jean-Pierre Chevenement was more reluctant to become heavily involved in the Gulf crisis and imposed such a tight regime of command and control on the French commander in the region that major

operational decisions had to be referred back to the defence minister. It was a slow and unresponsive system that placed heavy demands on Lieutenant-General Michel Roquejeoffre. Nevertheless, the French fought well in Desert Storm.

The Gulf crisis found a divided Germany on the verge of unification. Domestic politics therefore loomed large to powerful politicians like Chancellor Helmut Kohl, whereas the issue of Kuwait was further back on the agenda. In addition, constitutionally it would have been very difficult for the West Germans to send forces to the Middle East in view of the widespread hostility to any form of German militarism. However, Kohl negotiated the obstacles by providing German assistance in other areas, for example, to NATO, allowing US units to redeploy to the Gulf, supporting the move of VII Corps (based in Germany) to Saudi Arabia and providing billions of Deutschmarks in financial aid. Smaller European nations like Belgium, Denmark, Greece, Italy, the Netherlands, Norway, Portugal and Spain provided some forces (predominantly sea and air) for the coalition but others, including Czechoslovakia, Hungary and Poland, were happier to offer medical support. Opposition in Europe was not hugely significant, though the Pope was naturally opposed to the use of violence to achieve political aims, and, in general, the member nations of the European Community supported the actions of the UN-sanctioned coalition of forces.

Further to the east, the Soviet Union under Mikhail Gorbachev made some difficult decisions in favour of working with the coalition. Traditionally, the Soviet relationship with Iraq had been good. Thousands of Soviet citizens worked in Iraq and the country had built up a substantial level of debt with the former superpower. However, in the interests of a better future relationship with the United States, Gorbachev steered diplomacy on the issue of Iraq towards the consensus in the United Nations.

Among the Arab nations, the issue of the Iraqi invasion of Kuwait was contentious and created more divisions than usual. The Gulf

Arabs were firmly behind the coalition effort, particularly, Bahrain, Qatar, the UAE and, of course, Saudi Arabia. This latter country paid just under $20 billion in contributions to the coalition effort, with Kuwait providing a similar amount. All in all, the countries of this region covered about 60 per cent of the costs of the campaign in exchange for a return to the status quo. Egypt, Morocco and Syria (less wealthy Arab nations) offered a significant amount of military forces to eject the Iraqi forces from Kuwait. Other Arab nations and peoples were more sympathetic to Iraq's plight. Jordan and the PLO openly supported or maintained links with Saddam Hussein. Iraq also found significant support among the populations of Algeria, Tunisia and Mauritania. In contrast, Israel under Prime Minister Yitzhak Shamir, had long been opposed to Saddam Hussein and was more than willing to use violence against his regime when it suited the Jewish state. Of all the nations outside of the coalition, Israel had the potential to split the alliance, particularly the Arab members, by becoming involved in the war against Iraq. Saddam had gambled that his Scud-missile attacks on Israel would achieve this aim (and nearly succeeded) but enormous persuasion from the United States kept Israel on the sidelines. Even so, Israel's influence in Washington was manifested in a proposal to send Israeli military officers to Riyadh to instruct the coalition on what targets to hit! Eventually this plan was watered down (much to Schwarzkopf's relief) to a specific list of targets, many of which simply did not exist, thus forcing valuable coalition aircraft to fly dangerous missions for nothing.

In Asia, Pakistan had demonstrated support for the coalition by sending approximately 10,000 troops to the region, but internally great divisions existed within Pakistani politics about this course of action. India, too, found the issue of the forthcoming war against Iraq a difficult political balancing act between appeasing the strong internal anti-US sentiment in Indian politics but at the same time constructing a pragmatic approach that

tacitly aligned itself with the greater part of international opinion. Remarkably, even Afghanistan provided 300 Mujahedin. China took a more balanced stance towards Saddam Hussein, perhaps reflecting its relatively low level of national interest (despite having just under 10,000 citizens in Kuwait and Iraq) in that particular region and its actions in the UN Security Council were, in the main, constructive. Japan eventually emerged, as a very strong supporter of the coalition but in terms of military assistance was constitutionally hamstrung like the Germans; however, it pledged approximately $10 billion to help finance the overall operation. Its regional neighbours, South Korea, and more distantly, Singapore, also sent medical teams, while Australia and New Zealand dispatched ships and transport aircraft. On the huge continents of Africa and the Americas, the Gulf crisis did not raise significant levels of interest. Specific African nations like Niger, Senegal and Sierra Leone sent light forces and medical teams. In South America, just one country, Argentina, sent land forces, naval units and a few transport aircraft to contribute to the coalition. Further north, America's neighbour, Canada, sent just under 2,000 troops and some ships and combat aircraft as part of its contribution to Desert Shield and Desert Storm.

The impact of the Gulf crisis and war on the Iraqi citizen is often overlooked in the post-event euphoria. Life inside Iraq had been getting worse economically before the invasion of Kuwait and the subsequent UN embargoes made conditions deteriorate further. Rationing had been introduced in September 1990, prices rose steeply and certain commodities like meat, flour and sugar became increasingly difficult to obtain. As in most countries in the Middle East, fruit and vegetables were some of the few commodities readily available. For the average civilian, the war against the coalition forces added a new dimension of terror to their already difficult lives. What is often forgotten in high-tech, precision air operations designed to disrupt an enemy's

Making Kuwait a safer place by removing the debris of war. Explosive ordnance disposal teams use explosives to destroy mines and unexploded munitions. (Topham Picturepoint)

centre of gravity and their ability to control their military forces is that targets such as bridges, telecommunications and power stations are essential to the civilian population as well as to the military. Civilians spent weeks without regular electricity and water supplies and this greatly heightened the risk of infectious diseases. The coalition air campaign specifically focused on targets of military significance but inevitably generated what is known as 'collateral damage' or hits on unintended targets. Around 2,500 civilians were killed by coalition air strikes with approximately 6,000 wounded as well. The most serious incident occurred when a bomb hit a suspected command shelter called Al-Firdos on 13 February and was claimed to have killed over 200 civilians (mainly women and children) who were seeking protection from the bombing. For the conscripted military recruit, life was equally unpleasant and for those facing the coalition forces in the desert, the horrendous B-52 strikes (dropping bombs from 5 miles (8 km) above their targets) generated fear and panic as well as mass desertions. Many coalition soldiers captured Iraqi troops whose officers had cut their Achilles' tendons to prevent them from running away and in order to force them to fight.

In Kuwait, the conditions facing civilians were those of a population enduring a brutal occupation by a callous military force. The Iraqi forces called Kuwait the '19th province' and much of the initial take-over was characterised by a great deal of looting. In fact, many Iraqis tried to take their loot with them on their retreat down the road to Basra in late February but much of it was destroyed by coalition air power. Certainly, for the average Kuwaiti citizen who was forced to accept the presence of Iraqi troops, the six months under Saddam's control was a very frightening and mentally scarring experience. It is claimed that over 2,000

Kuwaitis died in this period and certainly thousands were forcibly sent to Iraq as well. For children, it was particularly disorientating, especially when fathers and elder brothers (the bedrock of family life in Arabia) were hauled away by the Iraqi military forces. Young boys would pelt passing Iraqi soldiers or tanks with stones and receive bullets in reply – a desperate cycle of violence that would remain etched in many young memories ten years later. Most significantly, the last acts of Saddam's forces can be categorised as a form of economic and environmental terrorism – setting fire to over 700 of Kuwait's oil wells – the effects of which, financially and in terms of health (from inhaling the noxious smoke), would be felt by the Kuwaiti population for many years after the conflict.

The UN, under the direction of Secretary-General Javier Perez de Cuellar, played a pivotal role in the negotiations with Iraq and ultimately sanctioned the use of force to liberate Kuwait. The United States, like Britain after Suez in 1956, had learnt in Vietnam that international support for the use of military assets was an essential requirement. The UN passed 15 Security Council resolutions between August 1990 and April 1991 concerning Iraq and its behaviour in the region. Initially, it was hoped that the embargoes and sanctions (notably UNSCR 661 and 670) which had reduced the income of Iraq's exports by over 90 per cent and halted all forms of international credit, would provoke the appropriate responses, but sadly they did not. The other major issue was that of foreign nationals in Kuwait (estimates suggest around 1 million in total) some of whom were seized as hostages. This produced one of the most terrifying media images of the war when Saddam was filmed talking with a young British hostage called Stuart Lockwood. All hostages were eventually released in batches by 15 December. The UN resolutions lent international legitimacy to what was clearly an undeclared limited war between Iraq and the coalition forces, to the extent of even

providing a timetable for conflict with
UNSCR 678 – in effect, a deadline for
the withdrawal of the occupying forces
in Kuwait.

The war against Iraq heralded a new type
of media experience: 24-hour war coverage,
which seemed to bring the civilian observer
around the world closer to the action than
ever before. But in fact this impression was
more illusory than real because the media
faced extremely stringent management by
the military – a hallmark of modern
operations. The vast majority of images of
bombs hitting targets were supplied by the
military themselves so observers were
watching filtered information. In addition,
all press teams had an escort officer who
monitored what was filmed and who
intervened if sensitive issues were raised.
Nevertheless, leaks occurred and
information that should not have got out
(like the ground offensive battle plan) did
get out. CNN became an international
phenomenon virtually overnight and
illustrated the power of modern satellite
communication systems in transmitting
live images globally. The Gulf War
demonstrated that the media are very much
major participants in a crisis and CNN has
become the reference channel for all parties
engaged in any international incident.
Certain journalists also made their name in
the Gulf War; to name just a few, Peter
Arnett of CNN who interviewed Saddam
Hussein in late January 1991, the BBC's
John Simpson who watched Tomahawk
missiles fly down the streets of Baghdad,
and his colleague, Kate Adie, who reported
on British troops in Saudi Arabia.

Another facet of the media frenzy in the
Gulf region, with approximately 1,500
reporters in Saudi Arabia alone, was the ease
with which Iraq could use the media for
propaganda purposes. The capture of allied
air crews whose planes were shot down
attacking Iraqi targets added a new
dimension to the military campaign.
Unedited footage of bruised pilots who had
endured torture at the hands of the Iraqis
and now were forced to read prepared

The propaganda tapes of the captured
Tornado aircrew, John Peters and John
Nichol, shocked many people around
the world. Both men, Peters in
particular, were badly bruised and clearly
forced to read prepared statements
condemning the war. All of this
horrendous treatment violated the
Geneva conventions about the handling
of prisoners of war.

statements condemning the war had a
profound impact on world viewers. The
images of the war suddenly changed from
representing a one-sided affair to conveying
an enemy who had the capability to shoot
down multi-million-dollar aircraft and force
their crews to say anything. The appearance
on television of the downed British Tornado
crew, John Peters and John Nichol, was a
particularly disturbing image, with their
bruised faces and dispirited demeanours.
These pictures reinforced the widespread
notion that Iraq did not treat prisoners of
war in accordance with the Geneva
conventions and raised great concerns
about the fate of captured personnel
(mainly aircrew and Special Forces). The
potential for disruption of the coalition
efforts by these pictures was recognised due
to their impact on civilian morale on the
home front. Just two years later, the images
of dead American soldiers being dragged
through the streets of Mogadishu by a mob
of angry Somalis would effectively end the
US operations in that country. One of the
most significant features of this 'body bag'-
sensitive campaign in the Gulf was the
virtual absence of imagery depicting dead
coalition soldiers in explicit contrast to
Vietnam. Ironically, towards the end of the
ground offensive, fears among those in the
press of mounting Iraqi casualties put
pressure on the Bush administration to end
the hostilities as quickly as possible,
revealing the fine line between a desired
decisive military victory and the
unwelcome charge of excessive slaughter.

Interestingly, the Gulf War enabled thousands of young American soldiers to experience the unexpected and rarely reported side of Arab culture: the enormous generosity to strangers, regardless of religion or skin colour. Saudi Arabia possesses the holiest sites in Islam, yet thousands of non-Muslim servicemen and women were welcomed into their land. The sight of women carrying weapons and wearing T-shirts (women in Saudi culture are not allowed to show their naked arms) caused a few ruffled feathers but nothing that was insurmountable. American soldiers whose vehicles had broken down in the desert would be astonished to receive meals from very grateful passing Saudi citizens. Children from villages would mob coalition soldiers and village elders would give the hot troops cold drinks (often Coca-Cola!).

And coalition mail that had considerable potential for containing contraband in the form of *Playboy* magazines, for example, received just a cursory glance from Saudi officials at the height of the campaign. In the deserts, coalition forces developed a respectful relationship with the hardy Bedouin who lived in that harsh environment. US tanks would manoeuvre delicately around the nomadic people when on exercise or occasionally during the heat of battle when they were caught between the warring sides. The Gulf War provided a rare moment in international relations in which Muslims and Christians looked beyond the Hollywood/media-driven stereotypes, realised that the 'other' was not so different and found common ground in the hot sands of Arabia.

Dina's story

The Iraqi invasion of Kuwait came as a complete surprise to ordinary Kuwaitis who woke up to a new and brutal regime after the Iraqi military machine launched its assault on 2 August 1990. One such person was Dina, an American from Nebraska in her early 30s who had married Ali, a Kuwaiti citizen, ten years previously. They had met while Ali was studying for a college degree in America, now had five children and lived on the coast of Kuwait in a city called Rumaithiya. Like many Kuwaitis, they lived together with Ali's parents and brothers in a three-storey building that was divided into separate apartments. The initial reaction to the sounds of bombs being dropped by Iraqi warplanes and machine-gun fire in the early morning was utter confusion. Nobody knew what was going on, television screens were blank and Kuwaiti radio stations just played national songs, all of which added to the widespread ignorance of the unfolding events. Those that tuned into Iraqi radio stations heard propaganda which announced that the Kuwaitis had 'invited in' the Iraqi forces to overthrow the government. Total confusion faced the average Kuwaiti. Some people even found themselves going to work, no doubt in some bewildered hope that everything was normal after all.

The first real indications of the magnitude of the disaster facing Kuwait came by word of mouth from those who had witnessed the thousands of Iraqi troops and tanks rolling through Kuwait. Dina was first made aware of their presence by a hysterical phone call from her sister-in-law who lived outside of Rumaithiya. Her first reaction on hearing the news was to throw up in the bathroom in fear of what would happen to her and her children. As with all Arab families, the most important decision-maker and adviser is the father and Ali's father, Eidan, believed that

this would blow over very quickly because Kuwait had not experienced a war for many years and the Iraqis could not seriously think that Kuwait's neighbours would accept the invasion. For the women of the family, the initial response was less optimistic and more practical – find food and stock up in case the crisis lasted a long time. Many shops were emptied quickly not by Kuwaitis but by the Iraqi invaders who immediately shipped the food back to Iraq. Conditions in Iraq under Saddam had become very bad and soldiers took the opportunity to loot as much as possible at the very least to feed themselves. The widespread effect of the pillaging of Kuwait produced dramatic results overnight. Rubbish was no longer collected because the Iraqis had stolen the trucks. Piles of litter built up in once spotless streets, generating decay and a risk of disease. Bodies in the streets from the fighting and those in the morgues from the interrogation centres were also a significant problem. Many of the grave-diggers were foreigners and had fled the country after the invasion so ordinary Kuwaitis would have to sneak out after curfew to dig graves.

Life in occupied Kuwait

Living in a country that has been occupied by foreign soldiers and under placed curfew is a brutal experience. The first victim is freedom and Dina increasingly found herself locked inside her building with her children and Ali's family. In itself, this feeling of captivity (so unusual for westerners and Kuwaitis alike) and the fear of the 'knock on the door' created immense stress. In other parts of Kuwait, the initial reactions of the average citizen, a day after the shock of the Iraqi invasion had worn off, was to demonstrate in the streets. They soon learnt that the Iraqi reaction to such expressions of unhappiness was lethal: firing bullets into the crowd killing and wounding several people regardless of gender. Saddam quickly established his forces throughout the small country and people learnt to fear the secret police and intelligence officers who were the most brutal. Iraq's occupation of Kuwait was characterised by random acts of violence towards the population. Soldiers would shoot men for their cars and throw their bodies to the side of the road. Rape (a rare and abhorrent practice to Muslims) became commonplace, with soldiers breaking into houses to violate women. Rape was also often used to torture female prisoners. Suspected resistance fighters endured inconceivable barbarity at the hands of skilled Iraqi interrogators who used electric drills, acid and knives, among other things, to obtain confessions. Often innocent people having survived such depravity would be taken home and shot in front of their families as a warning to others. Some Kuwaitis collaborated with the new rulers but others, the majority, formed a resistance movement that either attacked vulnerable Iraqi soldiers or actively worked with forces in Saudi Arabia to undermine the Iraqi occupation. Several members of the resistance were foreign workers who had been caught up in the crisis.

For Dina and her extended family, having a foreigner in the building was an additional worry. Saddam used westerners as hostages in the initial stages of the crisis. Dina avoided being singled out as a foreigner by wearing a *hejab* (a headscarf) and, being very dark in skin colour, pretended to be a Kuwaiti. The pressure and fear took their toll on her in various ways. Her nerves were extremely fraught, especially with the sound of gunfire near the building, and she lost 20 lb (9 kg) in weight. Life in the first few weeks of the occupation was extremely difficult due to the uncertainty about the future. The international community was swift to condemn the invasion of Kuwait

but Kuwaitis realised that forcible removal of the Iraqi forces would not occur overnight. In the United States, Dina's parents were also deeply concerned about the welfare of their daughter and urged her to get on a flight to America which Saddam had authorised for all the remaining westerners from September onwards. Dina was persuaded twice to put her name on the flight but on both occasions, she refused to leave Ali. By early October, her family in Kuwait were so concerned about the state of Dina's health in view of her weight loss that they forced her to take a flight with her children back to the United States.

Escaping the madness

The process of leaving Kuwait was a frightening experience in itself. Dina and her children had to go to a central collection point in Kuwait and board a bus for Basra. The fear of being stopped and arrested by Iraqi officials on any pretext was at the forefront of her mind as the bus drove through the shambles of what had been Kuwait. Burnt-out vehicles, buildings and litter scattered everywhere dominated her view of the Kuwaiti landscape from the bus. After an extended wait in Basra, they took a plane to Baghdad Airport where they were met by welcoming US Embassy staff before taking the flight to London. From London, Dina and her children took another flight and arrived safely in the United States on 13 October. A few weeks after her arrival, Dina was debriefed by the US military or, more precisely, the Office of Special Investigation, who possessed a map of Kuwait that was so detailed she could identify her family home in Kuwait. The questions concerned the deployment of Iraqi forces in the city and other military matters, many of which Dina could not answer because she had not left her home from the beginning of the occupation.

Back in Kuwait, Ali was also deeply concerned about the fate of his wife and children but eventually got word that they had arrived safely in the United States. Certainly, in the weeks and months leading up to Desert Storm, Iraq's grip on Kuwait became more and more brutal. The hunt for resistance fighters was stepped up and Iraqi soldiers would use any excuse to round up Kuwaiti citizens for 'interrogation'. Nowhere was exempt from the searches, which included mosques and even maternity wards in hospitals. Men and women alike were brutalised by the Iraqi regime in its endeavours to root out the resistance, with many simply being tortured and/or summarily executed. The psychological effect of this treatment is still evident in many of its victims in Kuwait today. When the air offensive broke out, Saddam employed a different tactic, using Iraqi soldiers to round up Kuwaiti men to be transported back to Iraq as hostages. Medical treatment for Kuwaitis under Iraqi occupation was hard to obtain after the widespread ransacking of hospital medical supplies by the occupying forces in which everything was pillaged, from medicines through to expensive equipment. In human terms, a citizen of Kuwait counted for very little under Iraq's governorship of the country.

Freedom

The liberation of Kuwait from the harsh grip of Iraq only occurred after the ground offensive began on 24 February. Even then, the retreating Iraqi forces did their best to ruin what was left of the nation. The oil fields were set on fire and power stations were blown up in an organised fashion to create as much destruction as possible. As quickly as the coalition forces moved into Kuwait, the Iraqi forces began to retreat to Iraq, and Kuwaitis, at last, could feel free again. The liberation of Kuwait also generated several post-war problems: the issue of collaborators, the Palestinians who had helped the Iraqi forces, and the thousands of Kuwaiti citizens who had been taken forcibly to Iraq as hostages. Luckily, Dina's extended family in Kuwait had managed to survive the occupation without loss and Ali, who was desperate to see Dina again, took a flight from the UAE to the United States in mid-March, just weeks after the liberation.

Dina and Ali returned to Kuwait in late July 1991 and helped to rebuild the shattered country that was damaged both physically and psychologically by the brutal occupation. Dina is currently a teacher in a local school and Ali is a librarian in a nearby high school.

Ending hostilities

It rapidly became clear to military leaders and senior politicians of the coalition within a few days of the beginning of the ground offensive that the war for Kuwait was effectively won. The predictions of weeks and months of fighting had been dispelled by the ease with which Iraqi forces were neutralised by the advancing forces with remarkably few casualties. To a degree, the coalition forces were victims of mirror-imaging by taking the sheer size of Iraq's military forces at face value and judging it by western standards. In reality, the speed and success of the ground offensive was due to the fact that in terms of military equipment, most of the allies were at least a generation ahead of the Iraqis and in a completely different league with regard to military skills as well as their motivation to fight. By the third day of the ground operations, western planners and the media were beginning to suspect that a degree of overkill was creeping into operations. The road from Kuwait City heading north-west to Iraq became known as the 'highway of death' as it was littered with the burnt-out vehicles and charred corpses of those who had been trying desperately to get out of the Kuwaiti theatre of operations. Footage from Apache helicopters attacking road convoys showed the helicopters engaging individual soldiers running away from burnt vehicles with 30 mm cannon designed to destroy light armour. These factors persuaded President Bush to take the decision to suspend the fighting at 8.00 am on 28 February, at the 100-hour mark, to prevent excessive Iraqi casualties, which would inevitably have generated international condemnation and turned the memory of a famous military victory into a seriously unequal contest.

The last battle with the Hammurabi Division

Coalition forces continued to manoeuvre and fight (in the case of XVIII and VII Corps) until 8.00 am the next day to improve the strategic position. Schwarzkopf stipulated the need to destroy as much Iraqi equipment as possible in order to ensure that Iraq was neutralised as a regional threat for many years in the future. The last action took place after an unexpected clash between the 24th Infantry Division (Mechanised) and the Hammurabi Division on 2 March. The final position of the 24th Infantry Division (Mechanised) by the time of the suspension of fighting placed it just a couple of miles away from the Iraqi division, which had been trying to escape across the damaged causeway over the Hawr Al Hammar. By 2 March, the Hammurabi Division had managed to repair enough of the causeway to attempt a crossing but needed to fight through the positions of the 24th Infantry Division (Mechanised) to escape. Attacking the 1st Brigade of the American division provoked a fearsome response that was supplemented by artillery, MLRS and Apache helicopters. By the end of the fighting, nearly 200 Iraqi armoured vehicles and hundreds of trucks had been destroyed. The Hammurabi Division itself was severely mauled with just a few dispersed units making it across the border, with thousands of soldiers captured by the 24th Infantry Division (Mechanised).

Ceasefire talks at Safwan

Several options had been discussed by Chairman of the Joint Chiefs-of-Staff Colin Powell and General Schwarzkopf about how

and where to hold the ceasefire negotiations
with the Iraqi forces. Given the state of the
battlefield, 'negotiation' was a broad term for
what was really a surrender by the Iraqi
forces. Initially, the battleship *Missouri*, was
considered a good option in view of the
symbolism of holding negotiations on board
a ship, which had been the official venue for
the Japanese surrender in 1945, but in
practical terms the preparations would have
taken a considerable amount of time to
organise. The second option was Jalibah
airbase, which the 24th Infantry Division
(Mechanised) had seized, whose location –
being just under 100 miles (160 km) inside
Iraqi territory – would, again, have possessed
additional meaning; in any case, the amount
of unexploded weaponry around the base
precluded its use. The final option, chosen by
Schwarzkopf himself, was Safwan airfield just
a few miles within Iraq from the Kuwaiti
border. CENTCOM's maps had clearly marked
the area as having been taken by the 1st
Infantry Division (Mechanised) 'The Big Red
One'. However, Schwarzkopf, having been
told by VII Corps that they had taken it, now
discovered that in fact no coalition troops
were at the airfield, and it was still being held
by a small force of Iraqi armour. In his
memoirs, Schwarzkopf recalls how the feeling
of being lied to combined with his frustration
at VII Corps' slow pace 'came boiling out' at
this stage and a frank expression of opinion
flowed from him to General Yeosock.
Subsequently, 'The Big Red One' was ordered
to surround the Iraqi forces with
overwhelming military force and issue a
command to leave. The Iraqi commander
sensibly decided to comply with the demand
after witnessing 50 MBTs, Apache helicopters
and mechanised infantry surround his unit.

The opposing generals meet over a table in the desert

General Schwarzkopf and his senior coalition
commanders met the Iraqi delegates just
after 11.00 am on 3 March at Safwan airfield.
Washington had given CENTCOM a

significant amount of latitude to handle the
negotiations rather than sending a civilian
expert from the State Department and, in
fact, Schwarzkopf was the senior
representative of the coalition. Saddam
Hussein sent his deputy chief-of-staff at the
Ministry of Defence, Lieutenant-General
Sultan Hashim Ahmad, and the Commander
of the Iraqi III Corps, Lieutenant-General
Salah Abud Mahmud. All personal weapons
were taken away from the participants in the

The talks at Safwan. (Topham Picturepoint)

talks and everyone was searched to ensure the tightest security. The atmosphere was decidedly cold as Schwarzkopf laid out his demands: access to prisoners of war by the Red Cross; immediate return of all prisoners; the return of the dead; the identification of minefields and unconventional weapons in Kuwait; and the need to deal with the issue of those missing in action. The number of prisoners of war led to an exchange of sharply contrasting figures between the two generals, with Iraq admitting to having captured 41 prisoners of various nationalities and the number of Iraqis captured by the coalition amounting to over 60,000. This figure shocked the chief Iraqi negotiator, General Ahmad, who had been unaware of the sheer scale of the defeat.

Three contentious issues arose in the meeting that would have significant consequences for the future. The first concerned the thousands of Kuwaiti citizens who had been forcibly taken to Iraq. General Ahmad denied this, stating that Kuwaitis who had gone to Iraq had done so voluntarily. This issue was never resolved satisfactorily and, though some Kuwaitis were returned, to this day, significant numbers are still missing. The second point of contention concerned the battle between the 24th Infantry Division (Mechanised) and the Hammurabi Division that led to a formal but temporary ceasefire line that encompassed parts of Iraq. It was recognised by both sides that in time the borders would return to their pre-war positions. The final issue was the Iraqi request to use helicopters to move around Iraq. Fixed-wing aircraft had been banned from flying but bearing in mind the amount of damage inflicted on Iraq's infrastructure, it seemed a reasonable proposition and Schwarzkopf acceded. These helicopters, including gunships, would be used in subsequent weeks by Saddam Hussein to put down rebellions through his territory. It was a clever ploy that the Iraqis exploited to the full. Nevertheless, their military forces had lost nearly 80 per cent of their tanks, 90 per cent of their artillery, and over 50 per cent of their armoured personnel carriers in Kuwait. It would not be possible for them to replace many of these military resources in the near future in view of the parlous state of the Iraqi economy.

The UN passed UNSCR 686 the day before the meeting at Safwan laid out the terms of the ceasefire. A month later, UNSCR 687 covered the issues of Kuwait's borders; war reparations; and the creation of UN Special Commission (UNSCOM) weapons inspectors to ensure the removal from Iraq of all biological and chemical weapons as well as ballistic missiles with a range exceeding 93 miles (150 km). For the coalition troops, the successful conclusion of the ceasefire talks at Safwan meant that many soldiers

were on their way home within a matter of days and soon over 5,000 US troops were leaving the Middle East daily. By January 1992, about half a million American troops had left the theatre of operations. The Americans returned to a heroes' welcome. Crowds of people were waiting for the returning aircraft filled with veterans of the Gulf War, many of them immediate family but others were people who just wanted to join in the celebration. New York and other cities threw traditional tickertape parades for the soldiers, sailors and aircrews and Washington hosted the 'victory' parade. For the commanders, the return was slightly delayed due to the pressing business of putting Kuwait back on its feet again. General Schwarzkopf moved his headquarters back to the United States approximately six weeks after meeting the Iraqi delegation at Safwan. America celebrated his return in true style. Schwarzkopf was the first high-ranking officer from the United States to have won such a comprehensive victory since the Second World War, and his rapturous reception was very different to that on the return of General Mark Clark from the Korean War and General Westmoreland returning from Vietnam. The victory in the Gulf War had restored a great deal of pride in the armed forces of the United States and society took the opportunity to rejoice. Awards and honours were heaped on those who had fought the campaign in the desert and, this time, 'Purple Hearts' – the medal awarded to those wounded in action – were not the most numerous. In other coalition nations, similar celebrations for their forces also took place, in Britain, for example, church bells rang out across the country to commemorate the famous victory in the Gulf. It was a time to celebrate and millions of people across the world were united by the common perception that their country had in some way helped eject a brutal dictator from an occupied nation.

Casualties

The Gulf War of 1991 stands out in the annals of warfare in the 20th century because of the staggeringly low number of combat casualties between the combined coalition and Iraqi forces of well over a million military personnel. The United States lost just 147 killed in action (KIA), which makes an interesting comparison with the Korean War (over 30,000 dead) and the Vietnam War (just under 60,000 killed). The allies suffered 99 KIA of which the Saudis lost the largest number, 29 in all. The number of wounded is slightly less precise due to different methods of accounting but the consensus suggests that around 450 US troops were wounded with a similar number among the other coalition forces. Surprisingly, other causes of death and serious injury (accidents and illness) amounted to just under 1,500 Americans and even the British who lost 24 KIA had to withdraw nearly 700 military personnel from the Gulf due to illness or accidents. It is remarkable that the combat deaths and injuries are significantly outnumbered by those caused by disease and accidents. In fact, non-hostile fatalities during Desert Storm (especially friendly fire or 'blue on blue') accounted for a total of 152 Americans – that is, more than over half a million hostile Iraqis (or 250,000 depending on whose figures you use) could achieve! Placed in the context of past wars, there is unfortunately nothing new about friendly fire and it is likely to remain a permanent feature of any battlefield.

The number of Iraqi combat casualties is more contentious. A plethora of figures exists in the literature on the Gulf War ranging from 10,000 to 200,000 killed in action. CENTCOM puts the number at around 20,000 and contemporary research would suggest that this figure has a great deal of merit. The number of wounded personnel has also raised further debate, with suggested figures ranging from about 25,000 to over a quarter of a million. The history of modern warfare suggests that often double or treble the number of dead are wounded so CENTCOM's estimate of 60,000 may be the most accurate but, given the vast amount of desertions in the Iraqi Army, lower figures may be more pertinent. Reports of civilian deaths range from 1,000 to 15,000 and the Iraqi figure of just under 2,500 appears quite plausible within this scale, with approximately 6,000 wounded. A completely accurate picture of the number of Iraqis who died in the campaign may never be possible because of the lack of transparency in that country and the failure, for overwhelming political reasons, to obtain accurate figures. The publication of the true numbers of deaths, even if they are relatively low, would not enhance the popularity of Saddam Hussein's administration.

Short-term military and political victory?

In military terms, the campaign in the Persian Gulf was extremely successful. The coalition forces achieved complete superiority in the air, at sea and on land, with minimal losses. Iraq was comprehensively defeated in the Kuwaiti theatre of operations and in 15 per cent of its own territory. Politically, the outcome of the Gulf War is more contentious. In an immediate sense, Kuwait's stolen sovereignty was restored, the Al-Sabah family was put back in power and the UN's aims were fulfilled. But the regional threat remained. Saddam Hussein remained in power, despite earnest calls from the United States to different elements of Iraq's population, for example, the Kurds and the Shi'ites, to depose him. In fact, Saddam has politically outlived the majority of his opponents and contemporaries in the global political arena, including George Bush (Snr), Mikhail Gorbachev, Margaret Thatcher, John Major, François Mitterrand, Helmut Kohl, Hafiz Asad of Syria, Hussein of Jordan, Yitzhak Shamir in Israel and the UN's Javier Perez de Cuellar. So, what did the Gulf War achieve? A new international order in which the sovereignty of states and edicts from the UN would be respected or just a return to the status quo? The tragedy of the Balkans in the 1990s and the current crisis in Palestine would point strongly towards the latter.

Military lessons

A wide range of 'lessons' can be derived from the fighting in the Gulf War and these have enormous relevance for future warfare. First and foremost, the timing of the campaign could not have been better for the major participant in the coalition, the United States. As one soldier who took part in the fighting has noted, much of the success of the US forces in this war lies to a degree with President Bush but more so with President Reagan who had built up these capabilities during the Cold War. The armed forces arrayed against the Iraqis had been sharply honed in terms of planning, preparation and equipment by readying for war against the Soviet Union. By fortunate coincidence, the Cold War had ended just a year before and the United States still had a pool of trained forces to draw from in times of crisis. Had the Gulf War occurred two years later, it would have been much harder to rapidly deploy so many units so quickly and, as it was, a significant number of reservists (approximately 200,000 from the United States) also took part in the Gulf War. The quality of the military technology within the coalition made a fundamental difference in the combat effectiveness of their units. One factor that was apparent in the air, sea and

land wars was the ability of coalition forces to fight effectively at night. Night-vision devices like low-altitude navigation infrared for night (LANTIRN), forward-looking infrared (FLIR) pods for aircraft, thermal night sights like thermal and optical gun sights (TOGS) on tanks, and night-vision goggles for soldiers enabled the coalition to fight 'around the clock'. Such technology allowed planners to raise the tempo of operations to a higher level than ever before and the only inhibiting factor was the ability of military personnel to keep up with the pace set by the equipment.

A comparison of weapons shows a distinct advantage on the side of the better-equipped forces. In the air, coalition aircraft were simply in a different league to the highly advanced aircraft that the Iraqis possessed but hardly used. Stealth technology demonstrated a revolutionary ability to penetrate sophisticated air defences that Iraq simply could not counter. AWACS and the ATO offered a level of air management that facilitated one of the most successful aerial offensives in the history of warfare. The Tomahawk missile (both air- and sea-delivered versions) gave coalition planners a low-cost (human not financial) option to accurately hit targets deep within the enemy's heartland that was difficult to counter, especially at night. At sea, the critical value of merchant ships in moving the heavy land equipment and sustaining the ground forces was reinforced. The Gulf War was not an ideal environment for the powerful carrier battle groups of the US Navy but they and their partners played an important role in cutting off Iraq's seaborne options. The single most important lesson for the forces in the Gulf was the dangers of an old threat (mines) but fortunately the Royal Navy had maintained a significant mine-warfare capability.

On land, one of the major advantages that planners like Schwarzkopf possessed was excellent intelligence assets. The environment of the desert campaign lent itself to the acquisition of accurate information about the enemy. In space, reconnaissance satellites like the KH-11 and the Lacrosse radar-imaging satellite provided untouchable (by Iraqi forces) coverage of the battlespace. Other satellites carried the critical communication channels and equally important were those satellites that allowed the global positioning system (GPS) to work. GPS allowed unprecedented levels of accuracy concerning battlefield navigation that was so vital in manoeuvre warfare. JSTARS offered a previously unheard-of near real-time access to the overall strategic picture on the ground and its limited but extremely valuable role over the Kuwaiti theatre of operations heralded the way ahead for future commanders. On the ground, unmanned aerial vehicles (UAV) started to make a significant but limited appearance in the form of the Israeli-designed Pioneer system. Overall, these assets were very useful and supplemented traditional aerial photo-reconnaissance aircraft like the U2. In the contest of armour, coalition tanks like the American M1A1 and British Challenger were also a generation ahead of anything the Iraqis possessed. The most significant advantage is

that they could move and fire at the same time, which was something the enemy tanks could not do. Often in battle, Iraqi tanks would mistakenly fire at the muzzle flash of the coalition tank not realising that it was no longer in that position. The ability of western tanks to fire further, with greater accuracy and with more punch (using depleted uranium shells), proved to be decisive and the Apache helicopter demonstrated that the rotary aircraft was a major threat to armour on the battlefield with its hellfire missiles; the Iraqis had very little to counter this powerful war vehicle.

The Gulf states and the west

From a regional perspective, the impact of the Gulf War had profound strategic, economic and political consequences. The strategic price of accepting the intervention of the United States has resulted in a closer alignment of the Gulf states with the only

Aftermath of the Khobar Towers attack.
(Topham Picturepoint)

remaining superpower in the world. It is very difficult to ignore the 'oil' factor in America's decision to draw a line in the sand and then attack across it. In economic terms, Desert Shield and Desert Storm were both very expensive operations. The total cost of the campaign was $71 billion and countries in the region paid two-thirds of this cost. Furthermore, the relationship between the western nations and Kuwait, Saudi Arabia and the UAE has been characterised by substantial purchases of weapons since 1991. These have dramatically increased the overall cost of the war, and nations like Saudi Arabia have offered highly lucrative oil-for-arms deals to pay for the additional military capabilities. One consequence of these deals with arms companies has been an increased number of westerners in the region, mainly technicians, alongside the continued US military presence. Politically, this has generated a significant backlash (with global ramifications) in the form of violence towards foreigners. From the mid-1990s onwards, several incidents occurred, the most notable of these being the attack on the Khobar Towers carried out by Saudi militants, which killed 19 US service personnel. The most notorious of the new breed of Saudi radicals is Osama Bin Laden and his Al Qaeda network, whose attacks on foreign targets began during the late 1990s and culminated in the horrific destruction of the World Trade Center on 11 September 2001.

The unexpected effects of the Gulf War

One of the most pressing issues facing western nations who participated in the Gulf War had been the increasing number of veterans who have either died from or suffered mysterious illnesses since 1991. Increasingly, this phenomenon has become known on both sides of the Atlantic as 'Gulf War syndrome'. A variety of factors have been put forward as possible causes for these incidences, for example, the use of depleted uranium in tank shells and large-calibre bullets. When fired,

these rounds expel significant quantities of uranium during the process of leaving the barrel and then again when striking a target. Thousands of these shells were expended in parts of Iraq and Kuwait during the fighting. Recent concerns have led certain military organisations (like the US Navy) to withdraw depleted uranium ammunition from use due to fears about its safety. In addition, certain communities within Iraq have experienced birth abnormalities and higher than normal levels of cancer comparable with the experiences of some of the coalition veterans. Another possible cause of the 'Gulf War syndrome' illnesses is the cocktail of drugs given to service personnel to protect them from biological and chemical warfare. Many of these drugs had undergone years of testing individually but some questions have been raised as to the long-term effects of taking these very powerful vaccines in combination. A final possible source of the illnesses has focused on the Scud missile attacks on Saudi Arabia and the possible use of biological and chemical weapons by Saddam Hussein. It has been well documented that at least one of these missiles on impact set off chemical and biological warfare sensors but this was soon dismissed as the indicators were reacting to chemicals released by the high-explosive warhead itself. The questions raised by 'Gulf War syndrome' are now being investigated at government level in the west. Clearly all of these factors, whether considered individually or together, demand serious investigation.

Iraq, UNSCOM and no-fly zones

The end of the Gulf War did not mean that Iraq would be left to its own devices despite Saddam's apparent disregard of the international community when suppressing his own people, for example, the Shi'ites in 1992, or threatening Kuwait again in 1994. Crippling economic sanctions continued and UNSCR 687 set up inspection teams to investigate and remove Iraq's suspected weapons of mass destruction in April 1991. The following month, UNSCOM was deployed. UNSCOM faced enormous problems trying to root out Saddam Hussein's secret weapons and after six years reported to the UN that Iraq's deliberate policy of obstructing the free movement of the inspectors had severely reduced the effectiveness of the commission. The inspection teams were further hindered in their operations when Saddam expelled all the American members of UNSCOM, calling them 'spies'. US President, Bill Clinton, and the British Prime Minister, Tony Blair, took a hard line with Saddam over the issue of inspection and threatened the use of military force. The UN Secretary-General, Kofi Annan, tried to mediate with Baghdad over the issue of inspectors with a small degree of success, but in December 1998 the United States and Britain lost patience and launched Operation Desert Fox, a four-day strike against targets of predominantly military significance. The political cost of Desert Fox was the total refusal by Iraq to allow UNSCOM back into the country. The issue of weapons inspectors is still a hot topic at the UN today and in talks Iraq tends to link the issue with the ending of sanctions. In the years since the Gulf War, Britain and the United States have maintained no-fly zones over the northern and southern parts of Iraq to prevent further atrocities to the indigenous people (Kurds and Shi'ites respectively). During this very extended period, British and American warplanes flying regular patrols have routinely attacked radar and missile sites that 'illuminate' their aircraft, which has continued in the present day. The mandate for such actions is still very vague but they act as a reminder to Saddam that the attention of the international community has not completely left the region.

'Gulf War II'

The events of 11 September 2001, with the dual attack of the World Trade Center in New York and the Pentagon outside Washington, seem set to have a significant ripple effect in the Middle East. The new president, George Bush (Jnr), the son of the American President who launched Desert Storm, has declared a 'war on terror' that has resulted in the destruction of the Taliban regime in Afghanistan in 2002, the scattering of the Al Qaeda network, and significant military pressure on linked organisations, for example, Abu Sayyaf in the Philippines. The Saudi dissident, Osama Bin Laden, has become the most wanted individual in history but continues to evade capture or death. Attention now in the United States has focused on a 'regime change' in Iraq. President Bush's interest in Saddam Hussein is ostensibly tied to the possibility that Iraq as a rogue nation might launch some form of attack on America in the future using weapons of mass destruction. Beneath the surface, the President also has personal reasons for wanting Saddam Hussein removed because he tried to organise the assassination of his father (it failed) on a visit to Kuwait in the spring of 1993. In response to this discovered plot, the new President, Bill Clinton, ordered a Tomahawk missile strike (23 in total) at Iraqi intelligence facilities in Baghdad in late June 1993. But President Bush (Jnr) appears to want to go a step further than Clinton and remove the problem completely. Speculation exists that the United States plans to use a force of 250,000 troops attacking Iraq from three different directions with the focus of the campaign being the overthrow of the Iraqi leader.

Interestingly, the current obsession with Iraq has raised the old issue of why the coalition didn't finish the job in the first place when they had the assets to do it. But as Schwarzkopf reminds us in his memoirs, his mandate encompassed just the liberation of Kuwait; a subsequent push into Iraq would have split the coalition, particularly the Arab members. These arguments are very pertinent today. Many in the international community do not agree with the continued sanctions against Iraq and would clearly oppose a military assault. Furthermore, the reluctance of Arab nations to attack Iraq must not be interpreted as an expression of sympathy with Saddam. The overwhelming concern in the Arab community regarding

an attack on Iraq is the inevitable harm it would cause to the civilian population. It must be recognised that in all the years of UN sanctions and punitive actions by Britain

OPPOSITE The attack on the World Trade Center. (Topham Picturepoint)

BELOW George Bush (Jnr), who declared a 'war on terror' after the shocking events of 11 September 2001. (Topham Picturepoint)

and the United States (with significant amounts of collateral damage), the real victims have been the Iraqi people, not Saddam Hussein. This is the key issue for the Arab nations, and one that is likely to surface should the 'Gulf War II' take place in the near future. A decade after the Gulf War, the situation contains all the ingredients that led to conflict in the first place: a repressive and desperate Iraqi regime, an oil-rich region and a resource-dependent United States. Into this mixture has been thrown a fiery new element – international terrorism – which, ironically, emerged as a reaction to the continued presence of the United States in the Middle East after the Gulf War. The Gulf War of 1991 was a very limited campaign that merely reinstated the status quo in the region. The underlying causes of the Iraqi invasion were not addressed and in fact have been exacerbated over time. An international monster has been created out of a leader whom western nations were happy to support just six months before the assault on Kuwait. The United States used the Gulf War as a means to consolidate its position within this strategically vital oil-producing region of the world, but at the same time it has provoked a negative response by radicals in Saudi Arabia. The key question is whether a second Gulf War would address the regional issues that the first one failed to tackle – and would it dampen, or fan, the fires of terrorism that emerged in the aftermath of the liberation of Kuwait?

Further reading

Baudrillard, J., *The Gulf War Did Not Take Place*, Bloomington, 1995.

Bin Sultan, General K., et al, *Desert Warrior: A Personal View of the Gulf War by the Joint Forces Commander*, London, 1995.

Cordesman, A. H., and Wagner, A. R., *The Lessons of Modern War, Vol IV – The Gulf War*, Oxford, 1996.

Cordingley, Major-General P., *In the Eye of the Storm – Commanding the Desert Rats in the Gulf War*, London, 1996.

Craig, C., *Call for Fire: Sea Combat in the Falklands and the Gulf War*, London, 1995.

Danchev, A., and Keohane, D., (eds) *International Perspectives on the Gulf Conflict 1990–1991*, London, 1993.

De La Billiere, General Sir P., *Storm Command – A Personal Account of the Gulf War*, London, 1992.

Dinackus, T. D., *Order of Battle – Allied Ground Forces of Operation Desert Storm*, Oregon, 2000.

Freedman, L. and Karsh, E., *The Gulf Conflict 1990–1991 – Diplomacy and War in the New World Order*, London, 1994.

Geraghty, T., *Who Dares Wins – The Special Air Service 1950 to the Gulf War*, London, 1992.

Hallion, R. P., *Storm Over Iraq – Air Power and the Gulf War*, Washington, 1992.

Huffman, K. K., *Living the Nightmare – Escape from Kuwait*, Lincoln, Nebraska, 1999.

Marolda, E. J. and Schneller, R. J., *Shield and Sword – The United States Navy and the Persian Gulf War*, Washington, 2001.

Muellar, J., *Policy and Opinion in the Gulf War*, Chicago, 1994.

Peters, J. and Nicol, J., *Tornado Down*, London, 1992.

Ratcliffe, P., with Botham, N. and Hitchen, B., *Eye of the Storm – Twenty-Five Years in Action with the SAS*, London, 2001.

Schwarzkopf, General H. N., *It Doesn't Take a Hero*, London, 1992.

Vernon, A, Creighton, N., Downey, G., Holmes, R., and Trybula, D., *The Eyes of Orion – Five Tank Lieutenants in the Persian Gulf War*, Kent, Ohio, 1999.

Von Pivka, O., *Armies of the Middle East*, Letchworth, Herts, 1979.

Walsh, J., (ed.) *The Gulf War Did Not Happen*, Aldershot, 1995.

Abbreviations

AAA	anti-aircraft gun
ALARM	air-launched anti-radiation missile
ALCM	air-launched cruise missiles
ATO	air tasking order
AWACS	Airborne Warning and Control System
C3	command, control and communications
C3I	command, control, communications and intelligence
CENTCOM	Central Command
CNN	Cable Network News
COMUSNAVCENT	Commander US Naval Forces, Central Command
CTF	Commander, Task Force
CV	aircraft carrier
CVN	aircraft carrier
ECM	electronic counter-measure
EW	electronic warfare
FLIR	forward-looking infrared
FV	fighting vehicle
GPS	global positioning system
HA	heavy armour
HARM	high-speed anti-radiation missile
IR	infrared
JFC-E	Joint Forces Command - East
JFC-N	Joint Forces Command - North
JSTARS	joint surveillance-and-target-attack radar system
KIA	killed in action
LANTIRN	low-altitude navigation infrared for night
LGB	laser-guided bomb
LPH	landing-platform helicopter
MBT	main battle tank
MCM	mine counter-measure
MEB	marine expeditionary brigade
MEF	marine expeditionary force
MEU (SOC)	marine expeditionary unit (Special Operation Command)
MLRS	multiple-launch rocket system
MPSS	maritime pre-positioning ship squadron
NATO	North Atlantic Treaty Organisation
OPEC	Organisation of Petroleum Exporting Countries
PGM	precision-guided munition
PLO	Palestine Liberation Organisation
SAM	surface-to-air missile
TEL	transporter, erector and launcher
TERCOM	terrain-contour-matching system
TLAM	Tomahawk land-attack missile
TOGS	thermal and optical gun sight
TOW	tube-launched optically tracked wire-guided
UAE	United Arab Emirates
UAV	unmanned aerial vehicles
UN	United Nations
UNSCOM	United Nations Special Commission
UNSCR	United Nations Security Council Resolution

Index

Related titles from Osprey Publishing

To order any of these titles, or for more information on Osprey Publishing, contact:

Osprey Direct (UK)   *Tel:* +44 (0)1933 443863   *Fax:* +44 (0)1933 443849   *E-mail:* info@ospreydirect.co.uk
Osprey Direct (USA) c/o MBI Publishing   *Toll-free:* 1 800 826 6600   *Phone:* 1 715 294 3345
Fax: 1 715 294 4448   *E-mail:* info@ospreydirectusa.com

www.ospreypublishing.com

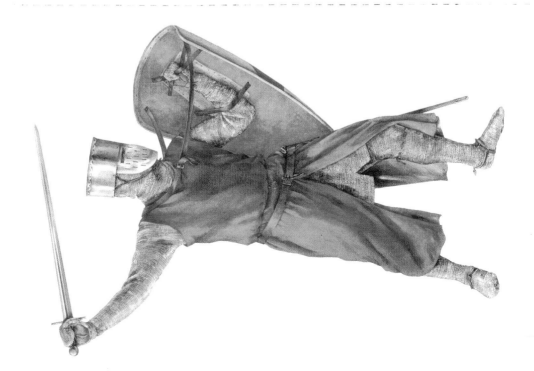

www.ospreypublishing.com

call our telephone hotline
for a free information pack

USA & Canada: 1-800-826-6600
UK, Europe and rest of world call:
+44 (0) 1933 443 863

Young Guardsman
Figure taken from *Warrior 22:
Imperial Guardsman 1799–1815*
Published by Osprey
Illustrated by Christa Hook

Knight, c.1190
Figure taken from *Warrior 1: Norman Knight 950 – 1204AD*
Published by Osprey
Illustrated by Christa Hook

POSTCARD